NOH
AS LIVING ART

JAPAN LIBRARY

NOH
AS LIVING ART

Inside Japan's Oldest Theatrical Tradition

YASUDA Noboru

Translated by KAWAMOTO Nozomu

Japan Publishing Industry Foundation for Culture

Notes on the Translation

This book was originally written for a Japanese audience. With the author's approval, passages have been condensed, supplemented, reorganized, or omitted with the needs and expectations of a non-Japanese audience in mind.

In general, the spelling of Japanese words follows the modified Hepburn system of romanization, which uses macrons to indicate long vowels. Exceptions are the word *noh*, for which the customary English spelling has been adopted, and certain common geographical names, such as Tokyo and Kyoto. Japanese personal names are given in their original order, surname first.

Noh as Living Art: Inside Japan's Oldest Theatrical Tradition
Yasuda Noboru. Translated by Kawamoto Nozomu.

Published by
Japan Publishing Industry Foundation for Culture (JPIC)
2-2-30 Kanda-Jinbocho, Chiyoda-ku, Tokyo 101-0051, Japan

First English edition: March 2021
© 2017 Yasuda Noboru
English translation © 2021 Japan Publishing Industry Foundation for Culture
All rights reserved

This book is a translation of *Nō: 650-nen tsuzuita shikake to wa* published by SHINCHOSHA Publishing Co., Ltd., Tokyo, in 2017.
English publishing rights arranged with SHINCHOSHA Publishing Co., Ltd., Tokyo.

Jacket design: Miki Kazuhiko, Ampersand Works

Printed in Japan
ISBN 978-4-86658-178-1
https://japanlibrary.jpic.or.jp/

Contents

Chapter VI

Noh and the Tapestry of Japanese Literature 65

Chapter VII

Engaging the Imagination 77

Chapter VIII

Why Study Noh?.. 83

Preface to the English Edition

One quiet evening in the twilight of his illustrious career, the pioneering playwright Zeami Motokiyo (1363–c. 1443) listened to a passage from his late play *Kinuta* and lamented aloud that soon there would be no one capable of appreciating such a work. History has proven Zeami wrong, for today *Kinuta* is counted among the masterpieces of noh, a theatrical tradition that has continued uninterrupted for some 650 years and continues to transport audiences in Japan and around the world.

Devotees of noh are by no means numerous, even in Japan. Today's audiences are generally made up of the same core group of ardent fans, many of them quite advanced in years. It is a dilemma facing all of Japan's traditional performing arts. Nonetheless, noh has survived far longer than Zeami could have predicted, influencing Japanese culture on almost every level.

One reason noh flourished throughout the premodern period was that members of the ruling samurai class were required to learn noh singing and dancing—less as a pastime than as a facet of their education and training. The study of noh nourished familiarity with the classics, insight into good governance, physical health and fitness, and empathy with the victims of war and other misfortunes. Noh outlasted the samurai, moreover, and its enduring vitality attests to its transcendent cultural, social, and educational value. My aim in writing this book was to convey something of this value to modern readers.

In these pages, I explore not only noh's history and structure but also its physical, emotional, and spiritual dimensions. To be sure, many of these topics have been dealt with elsewhere, in English as well as in

Japanese. What I offer here—perhaps uniquely—is my perspective as a professional actor specializing in *waki* roles. Most writing on noh adopts the viewpoint of the *shite*—the often supernatural protagonist, identifiable onstage by the iconic noh mask and costume. However, the *waki*, or foil, is equally essential, serving as a bridge between this world and the next, the medium through which the story of the *shite* is told. I believe that the *waki* viewpoint offers valuable insight not only into noh itself but also into its influence on Japanese writers and thinkers through the ages.

There is one important aspect of noh that I do not address at length in this book: the text. Noh is a genre of musical theater combining song, dance, and spoken dialogue. Most of the text is in verse, which is full of rhetorical devices and literary allusions that are apt to get lost in translation.

One common device is the use of wordplay to convey the emotions of the protagonist through descriptions of the surrounding environment. For example, cold gusts of wind (*arashi*) hurtling down a slope and whistling through the pines (*matsu*) express the pain of waiting (*matsu*) for a lover who does not appear (*araji*).

Place names are fraught with meaning as well. When we hear that the storm is taking place in Suma, where Prince Genji famously languished in exile, we naturally envision a desolate beach with waves crashing under a full autumn moon (symbolizing purity but also presaging emotional frenzy). Smoke rising from fires on the beach, where seawater is being boiled to make salt, is suggestive of a crematorium, hinting that the characters onstage are mere apparitions whose love has died long ago.

Such allusions and figures of speech are a challenge to translate into modern Japanese prose, let alone other languages.

There have been many valiant attempts to translate noh over the years, beginning with *The Noh Plays of Japan* by Arthur Waley (first published in 1921). While these translations are often remarkable for their meticulous scholarship and literary merit, few have succeeded in capturing the lyricism and layers of meaning conveyed by the original.

I am currently involved in a project to translate and publish (in the literary monthly *Shinchō*) ten noh plays, first into a modern Japanese vernacular that retains the poetry of the original and then into English. Partnering with me in this undertaking are Itō Seikō, a noted novelist and rap artist, and Jay Rubin, best known for his translations of Murakami Haruki's bestselling novels.

My hope is that *Noh as Living Art* will inspire readers to delve more deeply into the texts of noh plays, via the *Shinchō* series or other translations, and gain a fuller picture of this truly rich and vibrant art form. I am thus particularly grateful to the Japan Publishing Industry Foundation for Culture for selecting *Noh as Living Art* for inclusion in its Japan Library series of acclaimed Japanese books in translation.

PREFACE

I was twenty-four years old and working as a high school teacher when I went to see my first noh performance. I was very fond of music at the time, particularly jazz, but I knew next to nothing about noh and imagined it to be insufferably stodgy. Still, a colleague of mine (an art teacher) had an extra ticket, so I decided to go along. Little did I imagine then that I would build a career around noh as a performer, writer, and teacher.

The first play on the program, *Matsukaze*, literally opened my eyes to a new reality, for the bare stage before me magically metamorphosed into a beach in Suma under a glowing autumnal moon. I had never heard of the actors who appeared that day, but their performances left such a deep impression on me that I decided to learn more. One, as I later discovered, was Hōshō Kan, head of the Shimogakari Hōshō school of *waki* actors (of which I was to become a member). Another was Kaburaki Mineo, whose voice swept me away.

Determined to take lessons from a professional *waki* actor, I tracked Kaburaki sensei down, unaware that he did not accept apprentices. As luck would have it (or was it fate?) I knocked on his door just as someone else, a college student, was visiting with the same purpose in mind. Thinking he could teach us both at once, he relented, and we had our first class that very day.

I was teaching weekdays in northeastern Chiba prefecture but spending weekends in Tokyo playing in a band, so I began by squeezing noh lessons into my weekends in the capital. Over time, I became more and more engrossed in noh, until I found myself engaged in it full-time.

In retrospect, my first encounter with noh, my lessons with Kaburaki sensei, and my eventual debut as a performer all seem quite serendipitous.

There is an unfortunate stereotype of noh as slow-moving, esoteric, and inaccessible. I harbored the same image once, in the days when I spent all my spare time playing in a band. My aim in writing this book is to convey to others the magic that captivated me upon my very first encounter with this cultural tradition and the qualities that have continued to enrich my life ever since.

There has to be more to noh than the stodgy stereotype for it to have survived some 650 years. There are reasons why it was embraced by such rulers as Oda Nobunaga, Toyotomi Hideyoshi, and Tokugawa Ieyasu; officially sponsored by the Tokugawa shogunate; and patronized by leaders of the modern Meiji government. There are reasons why it fascinated and influenced such literary giants as Matsuo Bashō and Natsume Sōseki.

As I began digging into the history of noh, I learned just how important a role it has played in shaping Japanese culture and society. As a practitioner, I also gained a firsthand appreciation of its mental and physical benefits, as attested by the large number of professionals who remain active well into old age.

Slowly but surely, noh is attracting a new generation of devotees. They are drawn, as if by instinct, to the hidden treasures once jealously guarded by Japan's ruling elite. More than anything, my aim in writing this book is to encourage such exploration by shining a light "inside Japan's oldest theatrical tradition."

Chapter I

Keys to Noh's Enduring Relevance

Noh is a dramatic art form developed by Kan'ami and his son Zeami some 650 years ago, during Japan's Muromachi period (1336–1573). It has been performed over the centuries without interruption, making it one of the world's oldest living theatrical traditions. Noh was inscribed in the UNESCO Intangible Cultural Heritage list in 2008, becoming the first of twenty-one Japanese traditions to be thus recognized.

Shaped by the cumulative contributions of countless performances and viewings over the centuries, noh has developed into a precious resource that we continue to tap into today—much as layers of organic sediment have formed reserves of petroleum that enrich modern society in many ways. My long years of professional experience performing and studying this traditional art form have convinced me that noh is indeed a rich resource offering concrete benefits to contemporary society. I would group these benefits under five broad headings.

1. Insight into the sources of institutional (including business) durability and vitality
2. Keys to healthy longevity (as exemplified by noh actors who continue to perform in their eighties and nineties)

3. Stress reduction and a sense of well-being
4. Hints for effective governance and business management
   (as practiced by generations of rulers and corporate leaders)
5. Relevance of *mugen* noh (dream noh) to such advanced
   technologies as artificial intelligence, augmented reality,
   and virtual reality

I will return to each of these points in subsequent chapters, but here I would like to focus on the first in particular.

Institutional Durability and Vitality

Noh has been performed and enjoyed without interruption for 650 years, ever since it was established by Kan'ami Kiyotsugu (1333–84) and Zeami Motokiyo (1363–c. 1443). What are the keys to its enduring vitality? I would argue that they are the same essential qualities that have allowed so many venerable Japanese business establishments to survive for a century and more.

Japan boasts some 33,000 business establishments going back at least a hundred years. Of the roughly 5,600 businesses worldwide that have survived for over two centuries, more than half are Japanese. The rate at which firms enter and leave the market has picked up considerably of late, but those that endure have certain characteristics in common with noh, a theatrical tradition that has outlasted most if not all of these venerable commercial establishments.

What are those attributes? I would sum them up in two words: tradition (which is self-explanatory) and *shoshin*, which requires some explanation.

Shoshin, or "beginner's mind," is generally defined as an attitude of openness, similar to that of a novice. One of the best-known dictums pertaining to noh is an admonition attributed to Zeami: *Shoshin wasuru bekarazu*, or "Never forget *shoshin*." Most people today take this to mean something like, "Always retain a beginner's sense of wonder even after gaining technical mastery." But Zeami meant to convey more than that. Although the nuance changes according to context, the phrase is generally intended as an exhortation to never stand still, to continually discard the old self and create a new one.

The term *shoshin* existed long before Zeami, but Zeami assigned it a special nuance and a prominent place in the tradition and practice of noh. As I see it, the continual process of *shoshin*, paired with respect for tradition, has been critical to noh's survival over the past six and a half centuries. It is one of the ingenious built-in tools that have made noh such an exceptional and enduring medium of theatrical expression.

Embracing Change

Noh itself has experienced periods of *shoshin*—when it swept away the old and embraced the new—several times over the course of its history. I will outline four that have had a particularly profound impact.

The first was when the warlord Toyotomi Hideyoshi (1537–98) was at the pinnacle of his power. Hideyoshi was a great noh enthusiast and performed in many plays, including new works in which the protagonist was Hideyoshi himself. Until then, noh costumes were quite modest, not unlike the ordinary kimono of the day. But Hideyoshi, with his taste for the flamboyant, introduced exquisitely embroidered costumes of the sort that are still used today. The weight and stiffness of these ornate kimono restricted the movement of the actors and compelled them to develop new performance techniques.

Tokugawa Ieyasu (1543–1616), founder of the Tokugawa shogunate, shared Hideyoshi's enthusiasm for noh, as did Ieyasu's son, the second shōgun, Hidetada. Subsequently, noh was accorded the status of *shikigaku*, dance and music performed at official state functions, and it remained under the shogunate's sponsorship and control through the rest of the Edo period (1603–1868).

Noh's second transformation came in the first half of the Edo period. Sometime between the late seventeenth and mid-eighteenth century (under the fifth to eighth Tokugawa shōguns), performances became much slower and more stylized, decelerating to a pace that audiences today sometimes find sleep-inducing. Prior to this, the tempo is believed to have been two to three times faster. At that speed, noh sounds almost like rap music—and, who knows, back in Zeami's time, the movements might have been as lively as hip-hop.

The third big change came in the Meiji era (1868–1912), when performances began being held indoors. Until then, noh was performed on an open-air stage, forcing actors to use a booming voice and big, exaggerated movements. The construction of indoor noh theaters freed them to pursue subtler forms of physical and vocal expression.

The last major break with the past was in the period following World War II. Noh had briefly faced an existential crisis when the Meiji Restoration toppled the Tokugawa shogunate, its longtime sponsor. But it soon found wealthy new patrons among the peerage, the powerful zaibatsu families, and the Meiji political elite. After World War II, however, these sponsors were largely lost as well, and the various schools of noh had little choice but to charge admission and remake noh into a commercially viable performing art.

All four of these changes occurred quite abruptly. Veteran noh actors in the early Edo period may have initially balked at the new, plodding pace of performance. But in the face of changing demands, they put aside their misgivings and anxieties and made a clean break with the past, embracing the changes with an open "beginner's mind." Similarly, noh was forced to adapt quickly to the radically altered reality of postwar Japan. The innovations spawned by these changes exemplify the spirit of *shoshin*.

As living organisms, we are all changing day by day. Yet our self-image often remains stuck in the past. Human beings can be very resistant to change. But unless we update our self-image, the gap between image and reality continues to grow. Personal growth comes to a halt, and our lives become stagnant and stultifying.

At such times, we need to let go of what is nonessential and reclaim our *shoshin*, reconstructing our image of ourselves and moving on to the next stage in life. Zeami called this *jiji no shoshin*—shoshin at each new level of maturity. He also used the term *rōgo no shoshin*, or *shoshin* in old age, to indicate that the process of relinquishment and renewal should continue all through life.

To be sure, this is easier said than done. As we age, we become set in our ways and tend to fixate on past glories. We also become conscious of how little time we have left and grow fearful that it is too late to start over.

Zeami's advice is to forge ahead despite such anxieties, for life is always in a state of flux. Abandoning our old selves is admittedly frightening. We could lose our standing in the community. We might lose our friends or our savings. Our personal identity might crumble as our value system collapses. We might even go mad. But crises can also open the door to new opportunities. We cannot grow simply by playing it safe; we must take risks. Hence Zeami's advice never to forget *shoshin*.

Cracking the Shell

One way apprentices of noh are encouraged to break through to the next level—in the spirit of *shoshin*—is the *hiraki* system. A *hiraki* is one's first performance from a special set of plays that are considered particularly challenging. After mastering the basics of singing (melody and rhythm) and dancing (movement), apprentices are often offered the chance to perform one of those plays in a recital. (Amateurs may receive a *menjō*, or certificate, to confirm that they have attained sufficient proficiency in either singing or dancing to begin learning such a piece.)

In the professional milieu, a *hiraki* performance tests one's skills as an actor and certifies a certain level of competence, so one naturally puts a great deal of effort into rehearsing the piece. Unfortunately, it is not simply a matter of "practice makes perfect." In fact, the more you practice, the more impossible the role may seem. The challenge is not so much technical as artistic: giving expression to the spirit of the piece and portraying the character convincingly enough to bring its inner qualities to life.

Your teacher will repeatedly tell you that you are doing it wrong, but he will almost never explain how to do it right, let alone bestow a word of praise. At times it seems that whatever you do is bound to be unsatisfactory. In the end, you just want to throw up your hands and yell, "So, what am I supposed to do?" (Teachers are kinder to amateur students, of course, but even then, lessons can be somewhat bewildering.)

Perhaps the only consolation is the knowledge that your teacher, having given you this opportunity to perform a *hiraki*, must know deep inside that you are ready for the challenge. Indeed, it is essential to trust your teacher's judgment on the matter.

A common metaphor for the master-apprentice relationship is a mother hen and its unborn chick. When the chick is getting ready to hatch, it will begin poking at the eggshell from inside. But only when the mother hen pecks from the outside at the same time can the chick break out. The teacher is an expert at determining when it is time for the egg to hatch. Students should devote themselves wholeheartedly to rehearsing the assigned piece, knowing in their hearts that they have their teacher's blessing.

That said, breaking through entails a headlong leap into the unknown, in the spirit of *shoshin*. Preparation may seem like a long, dark tunnel, with no light at the end. Doubts linger, sometimes right up through the performance. You do the best you can, but invariably feel that you could have done much better. Still, in hindsight, you realize that the shell did crack. You have been born anew.

Ideally, *shoshin* should be an ongoing process of breaking the mold with each successive performance. Unfortunately, few of us have the fortitude for that. The *hiraki* system is a means of forcing us periodically to undergo a process of artistic death and rebirth, ensuring that we "never forget our *shoshin*."

Breaking out of the shell can be an exhilarating, cathartic experience, even for amateur students. Many practitioners become almost addicted to the thrill of *hiraki* and look forward eagerly to the next big challenge. This spirit of *shoshin* is surely a major reason noh as an art form was able to adapt to dramatically changed circumstances and survive a series of crises over six and a half centuries.

Now that we have explored some of the secrets of noh's adaptability, longevity, and ongoing vitality, let us briefly review its other gifts to humankind.

Healthy Longevity

The clichéd image of a noh actor is that of an elderly man, though in truth one will see people of all ages—including even children—backstage during a typical performance. Perhaps one reason for the stereotype is that many noh actors do continue performing until they are quite advanced in years. There is no age at which actors must retire, and most remain active throughout their lives.

We have entered an era of unprecedented longevity, and some believe that human beings could eventually live to the age of 130 years. The challenge now is to remain healthy and active throughout our long lives. Noh singing and dancing—especially the sliding style of walking called *suriashi*—exercise the mind and body in unique ways that may very well contribute to a long and healthy life.

Stress and Anxiety Reduction

The daimyō Oda Nobunaga (1534–82) was one of the three great unifiers of Japan in the late sixteenth century, along with Toyotomi Hideyoshi and Tokugawa Ieyasu. According to biographical sources, Nobunaga performed a short dance just before the decisive Battle of Okehazama in 1560.[1] In that battle, he defeated the 25,000-strong army of Imagawa Yoshimoto with a force a tenth that size in a daring offensive. On the eve of the battle, he must have been under almost unthinkable stress, knowing that defeat would mean certain death, not only for him but for his family, retainers, and allies as well.

The dance Nobunaga performed was about the Heike warrior Taira no Atsumori, killed when he was just sixteen. It was a piece that requires deep, powerful breaths to sing, along with dance movements that naturally balance the forces of yin and yang in the body.[2]

---

1. The piece that Nobunaga performed was not strictly speaking a noh dance but a closely related form called *kōwaka-mai*. Television dramas and other popular accounts have given rise to the misconception that Nobunaga performed the dance before taking his own life in 1582, during a coup at Honnō-ji in Kyoto.
2. See page 8.

By performing it, Nobunaga was able not only to calm his nerves but also to sublimate his anxiety into explosive energy.

Political and Business Leadership

During the Edo period, noh was a pastime enjoyed almost exclusively by the ruling warrior class. *Utai* (songs) from various plays were popular among the townspeople, but the general public had almost no opportunity to go see an actual noh play. On the other hand, members of the samurai aristocracy not only enjoyed watching noh but, in many cases, studied and performed it as part of their training and education.

Photo courtesy of Kinno Hoshi
(Photo by Watanabe Shinya).

A scene from the play Atsumori *(performed by Inoue Kazuyuki).*

This was a privilege reserved for a small, elite segment of society. In the Edo period, the warrior class is thought to have made up about 7 percent of Japan's population, and adult males belonging to this class constituted a mere 1.5 percent of the populace. These figures include low-ranking samurai, who rarely had the opportunity to study noh. Why was noh so heavily emphasized and jealously guarded by the ruling elite of Edo-period Japan? I will discuss this in greater detail as I examine noh in its historical context.

Relevance to Leading-Edge Technologies

One distinguishing feature of noh is the large share of plays with nonhuman characters. In fact, works whose characters are all living human beings—called *genzai-noh*, or "real-world noh"—make up only a small part of the repertoire. Most plays follow the *mugen* noh (dream noh) pattern, in which the protagonist, known as the *shite*, appears in the dream of the secondary character or foil, the *waki*.

The *waki* is typically an itinerant monk who, upon reaching a new destination, is informed of a famous local sight by the *shite*, often a mysterious old man or young woman. Eventually, certain hints alert one to the fact that this protagonist is no ordinary local resident, upon which he or she vanishes. In the second act, the *shite* reappears in their true guise—the ghost of a fallen warrior, a kami (deity), or the spirit of a tree or flower—performs a dance, and disappears as daylight breaks and the *waki* wakes from his dream.

The *mugen* noh form was one of Zeami's greatest theatrical inventions and is regarded as a hallmark of noh drama. Ghosts appear in plays around the world, but rarely are they assigned the leading role. As I will explain later, the unique structure and attributes of *mugen* noh have become a topic of research in the cutting-edge fields of artificial intelligence, augmented reality, and virtual reality.

With these points of relevance in mind, let us now take a closer look at the history of noh and its evolution over the past 650 years.

CHAPTER II

MYTHICAL ORIGINS TO FEUDAL TRANSFORMATION

The evolution of noh can be divided into four major periods:

1. Formative era
2. Flowering: the golden age of Kan'ami and Zeami
3. Transformation: development under Toyotomi Hideyoshi and other military rulers of the time
4. Crystallization: noh after its designation as the official theater (*shikigaku*) of the Tokugawa shogunate

In this chapter, we will explore the first three periods.

The origins of noh remain something of a mystery, but scholars commonly trace its ancestry to *sangaku*, a form of popular entertainment imported from China during the Nara period (710–94). According to this theory, *sangaku* eventually became *sarugaku*, the name by which noh was known before the Meiji era (1868–1912). Linguistic connections notwithstanding, extant illustrations of *sangaku* depict performances by acrobats and jugglers, conveying none of the mystery or spirituality that we associate with noh.

From my viewpoint as an actor, noh has more in common with native Japanese dance forms derived from ancient Shintō ceremonies in which priests, priestesses, or local worshippers channeled the kami

(Shintō deities) to confer blessings and deliver oracles. A good example is the oracular *kagura* ceremonial dance still performed in parts of Shimane prefecture. Zeami himself alluded to historical links between *kagura* and noh in his famed treatise *Fūshikaden*.

Up through the Edo period, "noh" was a general term encompassing various genres of performing art, including *sarugaku*, *dengaku* (derived from a type of ceremonial music and dance traditionally performed in farming villages), and *kōwaka-mai* (such as that famously performed by Oda Nobunaga; see page 7). Performers were organized into troupes called *za*. The four *sarugaku* troupes based in Yamato province (present-day Nara) are the ancestors of today's schools of noh.

Mythical Origins

Hata no Kawakatsu

In his *Fūshikaden*, Zeami attributes the beginnings of noh to a semi-mythical sixth-century figure named Hata no Kawakatsu. The legend of Hata no Kawakatsu also comes up in *Meishukushū*, a treatise written by Zeami's son-in-law, Konparu Zenchiku (1405–c. 1470). According to these two accounts, Kawakatsu was discovered as an infant in a jar that had floated down the river and washed up near Ōmiwa Shrine (in what is now Nara prefecture). Upon emerging from the jar, the child took possession of one of the people who had gathered around him and proclaimed himself the reincarnation of Qin Shi Huang, the first emperor of China. "I have something important to tell this country's rulers," the child announced.

Kawakatsu was taken to court to be raised near the emperor. His genius was soon recognized, and he was assigned to serve Prince Shōtoku (574–622), one of the most celebrated figures in Japanese history and the author of Japan's first constitution.[1] Along with many other accomplishments, Kawakatsu is said to have composed a piece

---

1. As imperial regent, Shōtoku issued the landmark Seventeen-Article Constitution in 604.

called *Okina*, which is still performed today. Unlike other works in the noh repertoire, *Okina* has no plot; it is more in the nature of a Shintō ritual than a drama. *Okina* is performed for the New Year's holiday and other auspicious occasions as a kind of prayer for good fortune. The treatises recount how such ceremonies brought peace and prosperity to Japan.

Eventually, however, Kawakatsu turned his back on life at court. Having transmitted his legacy to his children, he fled west by sea in a "hollow boat." He landed in a village in Harima province (now southwestern Hyōgo prefecture) and was pulled ashore by local divers. Instead of thanking his rescuers, however, he cursed the village, using his magical powers to wreak havoc. To appease this unruly sorcerer, the local residents built a number of shrines to Kawakatsu and worshipped him as a kami, after which he vowed to protect the village as its guardian deity.

Kawakatsu is said to have fathered three children, of whom one became a warrior, another a court musician, and the third a *sarugaku* actor. The warrior founded a prominent militia in the Yamato area, the musician became the patriarch of the Tōgi clan of court instrumentalists, and the *sarugaku* actor launched a line of noh actors.

Mystery of the Monkey

As I mentioned above, most historians trace the origins of *sarugaku* (noh) to the acrobatic *sangaku* imported from China in the eighth century. But the word *saru* (monkey) has associations with performing art that may extend even farther back.

Our main source for Japanese mythology is the *Kojiki* (*Record of Ancient Matters*), an eighth-century chronicle of the origins of the Japanese archipelago and the Japanese imperial line. The *Kojiki* describes two divine origins for the performing arts: the kami Amenouzume no Mikoto and Umisachihiko.

Amenouzume no Mikoto (revered as a goddess of art and entertainment, among other things) is best known as the kami whose bawdy dance lured the sun goddess Amaterasu from the cave in which she had secluded herself, plunging the world into darkness. Amenouzume is also famous for marrying the kami Sarutahiko and founding a line of female court dancers known as *sarume*, who performed *kagura*.

Tsubaki Grand Shrine in the city of Suzuka, Mie prefecture, and its roughly two thousand branch shrines dedicated to Sarutahiko all enshrine a *saru* kami with connections to the arts. In Chinese mythology, too, music and dance are said to have been invented by Kui, a divinity often depicted as a monkey. (One such depiction can be found at a Shintō shrine in Yamanashi prefecture.) Monkeys also figure prominently in *kyōgen*, a form of comic drama that evolved from the *sarugaku* tradition alongside noh.

Interestingly, Toyotomi Hideyoshi, the ruler responsible for noh's resurgence in the late Muromachi period (1336–1573), was nicknamed Saru. The sobriquet is usually ascribed to his simian looks, but there may have been more to it than that. Hideyoshi was called Hiyoshimaru as a boy, and Hiyoshi is the name of a group of shrines dedicated to Sarutahiko. It is fitting, therefore, that noh made such great strides under Hideyoshi, as I discuss in detail later in this chapter.

Wazaogi

The other mythical founder of the performing arts in Japan is Umisachihiko, the kami of the bounty of the sea. As narrated by both the *Kojiki* and the *Nihon shoki* (*Chronicle of Japan*),[2] Umisachihiko exchanges his chief hunting tool, a magic fishhook, for the magic bow of his younger brother Yamasachihiko (kami of the mountains' bounty). Umisachihiko later has a change of heart, but it turns out that Yamasachihiko has lost the hook. Furious, Umisachihiko refuses to accept the many gifts his younger brother offers as compensation. Searching in vain for the tool, Yamasachihiko finds his way to an undersea palace, where he meets a princess, the daughter of powerful kami. They marry, and Yamasachihiko's in-laws help him locate the lost hook. They also bestow on him the gift of two magic jewels that confer mastery over the tides.

---

2. The second-oldest official Japanese history, compiled in 720.

Ultimately, Yamasachihiko is unable to avoid a duel with his unforgiving older brother. But Yamasachihiko triumphs with the help of the magic jewels. Umisachihiko pleads for his life and repents, promising—as related in the *Nihon shoki*—to forever reenact his humiliation before his younger brother. He covers his face with red dye and vows to become an actor (*wazaogi*) for his brother's entertainment. In effect, the vanquished older brother becomes a court jester to demonstrate his subservience and allegiance to the conquering king. As this narrative suggests, actors were originally clowns—much like *kyōgen* comic actors—who survived by making themselves a butt of derision.

This view of the performing arts as something sycophantic and obsequious in nature prevailed until the fourteenth century, when Kan'ami and Zeami created a new art form free of such demeaning associations.

Zeami: From Beggar to Star

Zeami Motokiyo was born in 1363, the eldest son of Kan'ami Kiyotsugu. As a boy, he was called Oniyasha. His father Kan'ami was the leader and star of Yūzaki-za, one of the four *sarugaku* troupes in the Yamato (Nara) region, which were noted for their relatively realistic style of performance, referred to as *monomane* (literally, imitation). Kan'ami greatly expanded *sarugaku*'s artistic horizons, incorporating the elegant dances of *dengaku* and the intricate rhythms of *kusemai*, performed by female dancers called *shirabyōshi* for aristocratic patrons.

When Kan'ami's son was just twelve, the two were granted an opportunity to perform before the seventeen-year-old shōgun, Ashikaga Yoshimitsu (r. 1368–94), at Imagumano Shrine in Kyoto. Yoshimitsu was enthralled with the son in particular and showed him every sign of favor and affection. Indeed, the palace minister Sanjō Kintada scolded the young shōgun for rubbing shoulders with riffraff, saying, "Mummery is the behavior of beggars." But the boy's talents soon attracted the notice of others at Yoshimitsu's court, including the renowned poet Nijō Yoshimoto, who conferred on him the name Fujiwaka. By winning the favor of the shōgun and the aristocracy, Zeami and his father rose from "beggardom" to stardom, and noh became the entertainment of the elite.

After Kan'ami's death, Zeami took over as head of the troupe, which came to be known as the Kanze-za. He wrote many new plays and also expanded and revised older pieces, including those written by his father.

Zeami's chief artistic achievements were the development of *mugen* noh (centered on a nonhuman protagonist; see chapter 1) and the perfection of a unique style of musical drama built around the aesthetic of *yūgen*—variously defined as "unostentatious elegance," "subdued beauty," or "graceful refinement." In short, he solidified the formal and aesthetic foundations of noh as an art, while contributing many of the best-known plays in the noh repertoire.

While in his thirties, Zeami began writing the *Fūshikaden*, a philosophical treatise and practical manual for his successors based on his father's teachings and his own thoughts on acting. Zeami completed the treatise in 1418, when he was fifty-six. For many years, however, he had no children to whom he could transmit the secrets of his art. After finally naming his nephew On'ami as heir, he was blessed with two sons, Motomasa and Motoyoshi, and a daughter, who married the *sarugaku* actor Konparu Zenchiku. Zeami therefore reversed his earlier decision and entrusted the *Fūshikaden* to his elder son, Motomasa.

Zeami's standing among the ruling elite began to falter when a rival actor won over the affections of Shōgun Yoshimitsu. His fortunes declined further under the reign of the next shōgun, Yoshimochi, who preferred yet another performer. The sixth Ashikaga shōgun, Yoshinori, took a liking to On'ami, Zeami's nephew, and transferred leadership of the Kanze-za to him. This triggered a schism, with Zeami and his followers relegated to the status of a subordinate faction.

Zeami's misfortunes mounted. His younger son Motoyoshi turned his back on the world and entered the priesthood. A short time later, his elder son Motomasa died while still in his early thirties. Having lost both male descendants, Zeami decided to transmit his artistic secrets to his son-in-law, Konparu Zenchiku.

In 1434, at the age of seventy-two, Zeami was expelled from the capital of Kyoto and banished to the remote island of Sado, off the coast of what is now the city of Niigata. No one is sure why, but historians speculate that he was a victim of the rivalry between the Northern and Southern Imperial Courts. (Some, on the other hand, maintain that he was never banished at all.) According to the tradition of the Kanze school (descended from On'ami), Zeami died in 1443. However, the exact date and place of his death are uncertain.

Hideyoshi's Legacy

Although Zeami seems to have lived out his later years in relative obscurity, the theatrical art form he developed continued to win new enthusiasts among the elite. On'ami further boosted the status of the Kanze-za through his close ties with the shōgun, helping to cement noh's preeminence among the performing arts of the day. Konparu Zenchiku also contributed to noh's development by building on Zeami's legacy and authoring many plays in his own distinctive style.

By the time these two figures reached old age, however, the performing arts had entered a period of decline. The Ōnin War of 1467–77 thrust the country into turmoil, weakening the shōgun's authority. Journal entries from this period suggest that players were reduced to poverty, unable to afford proper costumes.

Leading noh's resurgence in the face of these challenges was On'ami's seventh son, Kanze Nobumitsu (d. 1516). His plays became very popular, and many survive to this day. Nobumitsu's oeuvre includes visually appealing spectacles like *Funabenkei* and *Momiji-gari*; myth-based works like *Tamanoi* and *Orochi*; and muted but highly refined plays like *Yugyōyanagi*, a favorite of the haiku poet Matsuo Bashō.

Also contributing to noh's rejuvenation were troupes called *tesarugaku*, made up of players with no formal professional background. These semiprofessional groups produced some outstanding performers and helped to broaden noh's appeal.

The Ashikaga shogunate effectively collapsed following the Ōnin War, opening the door to a century of warfare among competing daimyō. The fighting finally subsided with the appearance of three unifying conquerors. The first, Oda Nobunaga (1534–82), was a great fan of *sarugaku*. But the second, Toyotomi Hideyoshi (1537–98), was even more passionate about noh and had a far more profound and lasting impact on the art.

As a patron, Hideyoshi played a pivotal role in noh's evolution by financing the production of exquisite masks and gorgeous costumes and by commissioning many new plays—including some about his own military exploits. Six such self-adulatory works survive: *Akechi-uchi*, *Shibata*, *Hōjō*, *Yoshino-mōde*, *Kōya-sankei*, and *Konohana*. *Akechi-uchi* recounts in minute detail how Hideyoshi avenged the death of his lord, Nobunaga, at the hands of the traitorous Akechi Mitsuhide.

Hideyoshi was an enthusiastic performer as well. There is no evidence, however, that he was particularly adept at his art. In fact, records suggest that he was a poor singer who relied on "backup vocalists" to carry the melody.[3] He was a very busy man, after all, with enemies to conquer and a country to run. With little time to memorize his lines, he appears to have performed the same pieces over and over. There is an anecdote about a scheduled performance before the emperor that was ultimately cancelled, sparing the warlord a potentially embarrassing experience.

Hideyoshi invested lavishly in his hobby. I have mentioned the exquisitely embroidered costumes that came into use under his patronage. Another token of his devotion is a noh stage that can still be seen in the historic port town of Tomonoura in Hiroshima prefecture. Today, it is protected as an important cultural property and used only rarely, but I once had the opportunity to perform there. The dimensions of the stage itself are nothing out of the ordinary, but the backstage area is cramped. This is because it was designed to be portable; it could be disassembled, shipped, and rebuilt without the

---

3. Omote Akira and Amano Fumio, *Iwanami kōza nō kyōgen (1): Nōgaku no rekishi* (Iwanami Lectures on Noh and Kyōgen [1]: History of Nōgaku), Iwanami Shoten, 1987.

use of nails, so that Hideyoshi could take it with him wherever his conquests might lead. He may even have contemplated taking it with him to Korea, the target of an ill-advised invasion. It speaks volumes about his attachment to noh.

Hideyoshi studied with actors of the troupe that was to become the Konparu school—the oldest of the four existing schools—and even granted it a fief in Nara. But he was generous to the other groups (Kanze, Hōshō, and Kongō) as well, reviving their financial fortunes and enabling them to focus on cultivating their craft.

It is recorded that Hideyoshi enlisted two of his leading generals, Tokugawa Ieyasu and Maeda Toshiie, to perform with him in a *kyōgen* comedy called *Mimihiki* that spoofs the drinking habits and pranks of the common man. Ieyasu and Toshiie may not have felt entirely comfortable acting the buffoon on stage, but it was the kind of invitation one did not refuse.

Japanese historical TV dramas nowadays delight in portraying noh performances by Sengoku warlords like Date Masamune (who also excelled at drumming) and Sanada Yukimura. It is an effective dramatic device, but it also reflects a historical truth: By the end of the sixteenth century, noh had become a basic cultural attainment of the warrior elite. Hideyoshi played a key role in elevating noh to this status, setting the stage for the long and fruitful era of state sponsorship under the Tokugawa shogunate.

CHAPTER III

EDO PERIOD TO THE PRESENT

Development under Shogunal Patronage

The Tokugawa shogunate, whose rule spanned and defined the Edo period, was founded in 1603, when Tokugawa Ieyasu received the title of shōgun. Ieyasu had studied noh since childhood, which he spent in the care of the daimyō Imagawa Yoshimoto. Many of Ieyasu's dynastic successors were also avid students of noh. His son Hidetada (the second shōgun) was a noh aficionado known for his skill at the *tsuzumi* hand drum.

Although best known today for his love of dogs, the fifth shōgun, Tsunayoshi (r. 1680–1709), was also a particularly fervent devotee of noh. Tsunayoshi loved to perform, and he compelled many of those around him—including daimyō—to take the stage with him. Records show that Tsunayoshi even intervened in personnel decisions within the various noh troupes.[1] He also had several dozen noh actors elevated to the status of samurai, the ruling elite in a rigidly stratified class society. Noh had already received the designation of *shikigaku*—the dance and music performed at official state functions—under the

---

1. Omote Akira and Amano Fumio, *Iwanami kōza nō kyōgen (1): Nōgaku no rekishi* (Iwanami Lectures on Noh and Kyōgen [1]: History of Nōgaku), Iwanami Shoten, 1987.

third or fourth shōgun, but Tsunayoshi further strengthened its legal and social status as a state-sponsored art. From then on, a certain level of attainment became de rigueur for any upwardly mobile member of the ruling warrior class.

It was around this time that noh began to be taught locally in the domains. Contrary to what one might suppose, it thrived especially in provincial domains, such as Kaga (now Ishikawa prefecture) and Kumamoto, that were headed by *tozama* daimyō. These "outsider" daimyō, who had sworn fealty to Ieyasu only after his decisive victory in the Battle of Sekigahara, were consigned to domains that were relatively remote from the shogunal capital of Edo (now Tokyo), while at the same time being obliged to spend every other year in Edo under the *sankin kōtai* system. They were also under pressure to cultivate noh despite the exorbitant costs of assembling a set of masks and costumes and building a noh stage. (Indeed, the Tokugawa leadership may have used noh as another means of exhausting the financial resources of potential rivals, along with the *sankin kōtai* system.) Ironically, noh was less popular on the whole among the Tokugawa branch families and clans with close historic ties to the shōgun, perhaps because they were under less pressure.

One exception was the Matsudaira clan—related by blood to the Tokugawa—of the Matsue domain, in what is now Shimane prefecture. Matsudaira Harusato (1751–1818) was a particularly avid student of noh (as well as the tea ceremony). He even breached Edo society's strict class barriers to share his love of noh with the local townspeople. A contemporary account describes in detail how merchants and other commoners were invited inside the castle to perform as singers and musicians before the domain's leaders during the New Year's holiday.[2]

I mentioned in chapter 1 that performances slowed to around half the previous pace in the mid-Edo period. This probably took place sometime between the reigns of Tsunayoshi and the eighth shōgun, Yoshimune (r. 1716–45). Another major change was the development of a strong, rhythmic style of singing called *tsuyogin*, perhaps reflecting

---

2. Such episodes are recounted in *Ohayashi nikki* (Musical Diary), written by the Matsue merchant Takigawa Den'emon.

a preference among the warrior class for more powerful modes of expression. At the same time, a genre of action-based swordfighting plays (called *kirikumi* or *kiriai* noh) that had been popular prior to the Edo period largely disappeared from the *shikigaku* repertoire.

Because of noh's official status under the shogunate, the ability to perform it became something of a requirement among the samurai. But access to cultural education and resources varied by domain. This gap is humorously portrayed in a *rakugo*[3] tale called "Nō kyōgen" about a provincial lord who, after seeing a noh performance in Edo, is determined to stage something similar in his own small domain— despite the fact that none of his retainers have the first idea how. He ends up hiring two imposters from Edo, and the result is a comically bungled kabuki.

To a large extent, the seriousness with which noh was studied was a barometer of cultural conditions in any given province.

The Schools of Noh

In addition to Kanze, Hōshō, Konparu, and Kongō—the four Yamato (Nara) troupes that had been sanctioned by Toyotomi Hideyoshi (see chapter 2)—a fifth authorized school of noh, Kita, emerged in the Edo period.[4] Members of these groups were accredited as professional noh actors by the shogunate around the reign of Tsunayoshi, and the five-school framework established then is still essentially intact today.

The organization of noh is actually more complex, however, since separate schools exist for each category of performer (see page 24). In addition to actors specializing in *shite* (protagonist) roles, each performance requires a *waki* (foil),[5] *kyōgen* comic actors, and musicians to provide instrumental accompaniment (*hayashi*). The five *shite* schools are identical to the five schools of noh listed above. Of these, the Kanze and Hōshō are lumped together stylistically as the

---

3. A form of comic monologue involving two or more characters, performed by a single storyteller (*rakugoka*) using minimal props.
4. Called Kita-ryū, unlike the four older groups, which were still referred to as *za*.
5. See page 9.

kamigakari schools, while Konparu, Kongō, and Kita are known as the *shimogakari* schools.

Present-Day Schools of Noh

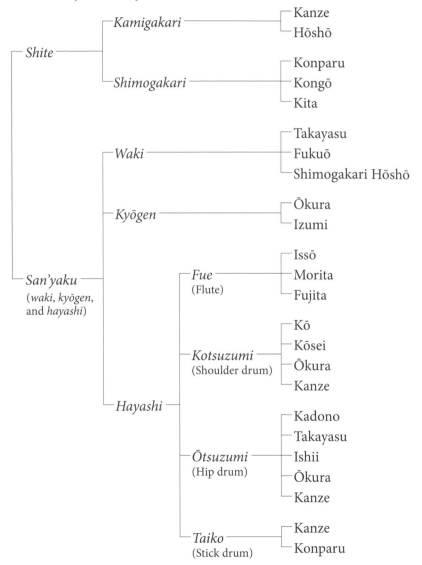

Source: *Manga de tanoshimu nō kyōgen* (Enjoying Noh and *Kyōgen* through Manga), Hinoki Shoten, 1996.

In the past, there were five *waki* schools, but the Shindō and Shundō schools have died out, leaving Takayasu, Fukuō, and Shimogakari Hōshō. Shimogakari Hōshō, the school to which I belong, began as an offshoot of Shundō, which was historically associated with the Konparu school of *shite* actors. My teacher's father was the head of the Shundō school, but he took his own life by seppuku (ritual disembowelment) on the day following Japan's surrender in World War II. The school was forced to disband, and my teacher joined the Shimogakari Hōshō school.

Inside and Outside the Official Framework

I wrote earlier about the semiprofessional *tesarugaku* troupes active in the late Muromachi period (1336–1573). In the Edo period as well, noh spilled outside the official framework. *Tsuji* (street-corner) noh was staged in public spaces or in small, makeshift theaters. This was noh without class pretensions, performed by people from all walks of life, including merchants and rōnin (disenfranchised samurai). There was also *onna* noh performed by women in the red-light district of Yoshiwara in Edo and the Shijōkawara entertainment district in Kyoto. These shows became quite popular, and the shogunate tried repeatedly to stop them.

Noh in the Edo period, then, can be roughly divided into four types: (1) the five professional schools patronized by the shogunate; (2) the noh supported by local daimyō, performed and taught by the apprentices of professionals in the shogunal ensembles; (3) Shintō-linked noh performed by local townspeople and farmers; and (4) *tsuji* (street-corner) noh performed by touring troupes and serious amateurs.[6]

An example of the third category is Sada Shin Noh, which is still staged today at Sada Shrine in Shimane prefecture. This is a form

---

6. As classified by Takemoto Mikio in "Edo jidai no nōgaku ni kansuru kisoteki kenkyū" (Basic Research on Noh and Kyōgen Performed in the Edo Period), a paper supported by a KAKENHI grant from the Japan Society for the Promotion of Science, 1990.

of *kagura* that acquired noh-like features over time, as townspeople who traveled to Kyoto brought back knowledge of noh from the imperial capital.[7]

Shimane is home to many ancient *kagura* traditions, including Ōdochi Kagura, which has been performed near Izumo Grand Shrine for at least three centuries. The backstage area is separated from the main stage by a street, literally turning the *kagura* into a *tsuji* performance, where everyday reality "intersects" with the otherworldly. This *kagura* is an offering to local ancestors, but its form evolved through contact with traveling noh troupes; the influence, moreover, appears to have been reciprocal. Mutual transformation is a frequent phenomenon in the performing arts of Japan.

The actors associated with the first two types of noh were accredited professionals with a status comparable to members of the Nohgaku Performers' Association today. Many local daimyō were eager to nurture such professionals to win the shōgun's favor, and not a few samurai became noh actors, which enabled them to launch a second career without forsaking their warrior status. For a talented rōnin, training as a noh actor could be a path to officialdom and stability. Still, those who wished to focus on their art must have found their bureaucratic responsibilities somewhat onerous.

Nonprofessionals and semiprofessionals also made a substantial contribution to noh's development, and some left an indelible mark. One such figure was Shimotsuma Shōshin (1551–1616), born to a family of Buddhist clerics. The warlord Oda Nobunaga valued him for his negotiating skills, but his life took an unlikely turn after he saved the life of a wounded noh actor. Shimotsuma took up noh and became an acclaimed *tesarugaku* actor, often outshining his professional contemporaries. Over a thirty-year career, until his death at age sixty-six, he starred in nearly 1,200 productions—probably more than most full-time actors.

Mention should also be made of Manabe Akifusa (1666–1720), who eventually rose to the exalted position of daimyō. Born to a provincial retainer, Akifusa started out as an actor, studying noh under

---

7. According to local residents.

Kita school founder Kita Shichidayū. His noh skills gained him the favor of the lord of the Kōfu domain, who later became the sixth Tokugawa shōgun, Ienobu (r. 1709–12). Akifusa served under the shōgun and, in 1710, became the daimyō of the Takasaki domain. He continued to serve the shogunate under Ienobu's son, Ietsugu, and became a pivotal government figure. Records of his accomplishments as a noh actor are scant, but his rise from such lowly beginnings to the highest levels of political power was a singular feat in the context of Edo period society.

Then there is Ōkubo Nagayasu (1545–1613). Born to a family of *sarugaku* actors, he served the Takeda clan and was eventually promoted to the position of retainer. Following the clan's demise, he was employed by Tokugawa Ieyasu, initially as a *sarugaku* performer. Having acquired mining expertise during his service to the Takeda clan, he was tapped to develop gold and silver mines for the shogunate, including those at Iwami, Izu, and Sado. (He is also credited with building the many noh stages for which the island of Sado is famous.) His legacy was tarnished following his death, as evidence of embezzlement and treason surfaced, but his life story is the stuff of TV dramas.

Utai in Everyday Life

After noh became the official theater of the shogunate and the samurai class, commoners rarely had the opportunity to view full-length plays. But they could still enjoy *utai*,[8] the sung component of noh. Zeami considered noh to consist primarily of *utai* and *mai* (dance), but he gave primacy to the former, since it carries the narrative.

Utai is based on a seven-five syllable count, a rhythm uniquely suited to the Japanese language. These twelve syllables are sung over an eight-beat measure when there is *hayashi* musical accompaniment, requiring some syllables to be held for two counts. The voice is not overtly adjusted for the age or gender of the character, and there is no absolute pitch. When performers sing in unison, they must follow the pitch and timbre set by the *jigashira* (chorus leader).

---

8. Also called *yōkyoku*.

The play *Yoshino tennin* begins with the lines, "Guided by banks of pale pink blossoms, I journey to the misty mountains of Yoshino."[9] Read as text, the words evoke little emotion, but when sung in noh's slow, distinctive style, they can conjure vivid images of Yoshino's wild cherry trees in full bloom, filling the sky with clouds of soft petals.

In *Unrin-in* the opening lines are "As wisteria bloom among the pines, I visit the famed temple called the Forest of Clouds."[10] Here, blooming wisteria is so resplendent that even the deep green pine needles and the clouds in the sky appear light violet. Such lines are most evocative when vocalized as *utai*.

This is noh as the townspeople of the Edo period understood it. They experienced noh not as a theatrical spectacle but as memorable or significant excerpts from the noh repertoire, detached from the plays themselves. In fact, these noh "songs" were integral to the social and cultural education of the common people.

Familiarity with *utai* began to spread as early as the Muromachi period, particularly in urban areas; by the Edo period, *utai* were an integral part of people's daily lives. *Utai* figured prominently among the textbooks used at the *terakoya* temple schools where the children of Japanese commoners received a basic education during the Edo period. The *utai* used were drawn from a variety of plays, including pieces based on literary classics and works with auspicious themes, from which short passages could be sung at weddings and other ceremonies. Taught alongside reading, writing, abacus, etiquette, and deportment, they entered the vocabulary of daily life. Not only wealthy merchants but even tradesmen like carpenters and fish mongers knew the auspicious *utai* appropriate to their trade. (In fact, even today, when familiarity with *utai* has become a rarity, it is fairly common to hear an excerpt sung at the ridgepole-raising ceremony for a new house.) And all guests were expected to sing such songs at weddings; if you could not, you had no business being there.

---

9. The Japanese text follows the seven-five-syllable structure: "Hana no kumoji o shirube ni te, Yoshino no oku o tazunen."

10. "Fuji saku matsu mo murasaki no, kumo no hayashi o tazunen."

A Link to the Classics

Until quite recently, people of a certain social rank or level of education were expected to study and practice the fine arts. The *Analects* of Confucius repeatedly stress the cultivation of the arts, along with the pursuit of virtue and "the way" (*dao*). Even today, Chinese literati can compose a poem on the spot, render it on paper in beautiful calligraphy, and often improvise an ink painting to go with the text. Some will recite the poem they have just created while playing the *guqin*, an ancient seven-string plucked instrument. This kind of skill was seen in Japan as well until forty or fifty years ago.

Cultivation of the arts was an educational tool in itself, deepening historical and cultural understanding and providing insight into ethical concepts like virtue and the *dao*. For the common people of premodern Japan, *utai* provided an ideal introduction to classical literature, which is so often quoted or paraphrased in noh.

Japan's literary classics are not about plot development so much as the deep sentiment, insight, and atmosphere of individual passages. These are best appreciated when read and recited over and over—ideally at spots or occasions reminiscent of the scene. *Utai* dovetailed with this orientation, being designed from the start to be spoken or sung aloud.

Even in the Edo period, few people had the time or opportunity to wade through a lengthy work like the early eleventh-century *Genji monogatari* (*Tale of Genji*). Their knowledge of the Shining Prince's escapades came mostly from the *utai* they learned at the *terakoya*. Many of the best-known chapters and scenes from *Genji monogatari*—such as those revolving around Utsusemi, Lady Aoi, and Lady Rokujō—had been developed into noh plays. In the process of learning the *utai* at school and reciting key passages written from the perspective of various characters, students would gradually gain a true appreciation and understanding of the work as a whole.

Noh as a theatrical production with elaborate costumes and finely crafted masks was a privilege of the warrior elite. But songs from these plays were readily accessible and popular among all classes, even in provincial towns and rural villages, providing a common cultural language spanning space, time, and class. The following anecdote is illustrative.

Early in the Meiji era (1868–1912), a lover of noh traveled to the city of Kanazawa and was walking along a street singing a section of the noh play *Hagoromo*. It was a scene where a fisherman named Hakuryō (*waki*) finds a beautiful robe hanging on a pine bough. He decides to take it home, show it to his family, and keep it as an heirloom. Just as he is about to walk away, he hears the voice of a young maiden (*shite*) calling out "Excuse me, but the robe is mine. Why are you taking it with you?"

When the traveler in Kanazawa finished singing the lines in which the *waki* expresses his intention to take the robe home, he heard a voice chiming in behind him. It was a local carpenter singing the part of the *shite*. The two ended up singing the rest of the play together and parted ways without even exchanging names. (Perhaps such an impromptu performance could only have happened in Kanazawa, the seat of the Kaga domain, where noh was so highly esteemed.)

It was Zeami's pioneering work that first brought literary classics like *Genji* and *Heike monogatari* (*Tale of the Heike*) to life on the stage. Collectively, *utai* constitutes a precious compendium of the best and most memorable elements of classical literature, local folklore, and *kagura* dances, as edited by Zeami and other playwrights through the ages.

Loser's Justice

It seems ironic, given that noh was initially patronized by the warrior class, but plays about famous military commanders almost invariably depict them suffering in Shuradō, a Buddhist hell where scenes of carnage are recapitulated endlessly. It is as if a bank were to sponsor art depicting the punishment awaiting avaricious bankers when they die.

The protagonist of a warrior play is most often someone on the losing side. A few plays spotlight victors, but they too are in hell, tormented by nightmarish scenes of battle. In either case, the play ends on a cathartic note, as the *shite* is lifted from agony and achieves nirvana,

Buddhist salvation. Such pieces must have functioned in large part as prayers for the peace of the vanquished and other fallen fighters.

A notable departure from this pattern is found in noh plays written during World War II. *Chūrei*, for example, recounts the tale of a soldier who is killed in battle but vows to fight for his country again when he is reborn. It is obviously meant as wartime propaganda and has little artistic merit. A 1943 play called *Miikusabune* is about a warship that is assaulted by demonic spirits but sails unscathed to its destination after the phantoms are subdued. The *shite* of this play, incidentally, is the kami of the equator; the *tsure* (supporting actor) is the dragon god; and other characters include the ship's captain, navigator, chief gunner, and deck officer. Quite a few noh plays of this ilk were written at this time.

The *mugen* noh form developed by Zeami was not oriented to glorifying war; it was far better suited to reflecting on war's horrors and offering solace to the victims. But noh largely abandoned this role during the modern era, as Japan strove to transform itself into a world power.

The Meiji and Postwar Crises

Noh faced its biggest crisis ever following the Meiji Restoration of 1868. With the fall of the Tokugawa shogunate and the abolition of the feudal domains, noh actors suddenly found themselves without patrons and were obliged to find other work to make ends meet. The head of one school took a position as a government clerk; other actors became street performers. Many noh stages fell into disrepair.

Noh might not be around today had it not been for Iwakura Tomomi (1825–83), an imperial court noble who was among the most influential figures in Japan's transition to the modern era. Iwakura worked tirelessly to revive noh, which he saw as an elevated art form comparable to European opera—and similarly useful as a means of entertaining foreign dignitaries. He arranged to have noh performed at his residence by the finest actors of the day (including those who had temporarily left the theater) during a visit by Emperor Meiji and his entourage.

In 1881, Iwakura established the Nōgakusha, a noh preservation society, with the new Meiji elite dominating its membership. It was Iwakura who coined the term *nōgaku*, encompassing both noh and *kyōgen*.[11] He also built a traditional noh stage that was encased within a larger building in Tokyo's Shiba Park. (The stage itself was later moved to Yasukuni Shrine.) Iwakura cared deeply about the construction of this theater and visited the site every day to monitor its progress. Most of the new theaters that sprang up thereafter were based on the Shiba design. The decision to keep all the trappings of an outdoor stage in an indoor hall was instrumental in preserving noh's distinctive theatrical tradition.

Emperor Meiji was a devoted fan of noh, as related in Donald Keene's *Emperor of Japan: Meiji and His World, 1852–1912*. The emperor built a theater for Empress Dowager Eishō (his lawful mother) in Aoyama Palace. The emperor's consort, Empress Shōken, also frequented the palace to attend performances there.

During the Edo period, professional performers of the five schools did not typically teach noh to commoners (although there were exceptions among *waki* actors). With the loss of their samurai patrons, these actors were obliged to begin accepting students from a broader cross-section of society. This helped to popularize noh among a newly affluent class of doctors, lawyers, and other professionals. Many literary giants of the period became enthusiasts, including Natsume Sōseki (a student of the Shimogakari Hōshō school), Masaoka Shiki, Takahama Kyoshi, Izumi Kyōka, and Yumeno Kyūsaku. Kyūsaku had students of his own and wrote many books about noh.

World War II ushered in another crisis. Young actors were drafted into the military, and it became nearly impossible to put on performances or conduct lessons. Many noh stages were burned in the air raids. In the immediate postwar years, noh actors made an effort to revive the art by touring schools across the country. There is also a record of a performance being staged in the year following Japan's surrender. But this was a time of crisis for all of Japanese society, not

---

11. This is the term inscribed on UNESCO's Intangible Cultural Heritage list.

just for noh. Later, as reconstruction proceeded, noh, too, made a gradual comeback.

In subsequent years, the appreciation and practice of noh as a theatrical form spread more widely among the public. Noh experienced a boom around 1965, following publication of Tachihara Masaaki's bestselling romantic novel *Takigi nō* (Firelight Noh). Noh by firelight was originally performed only at Nara's Kōfuku-ji in February, as part of the temple's *omizutori* (water-drawing) ritual, but it became a national year-round attraction after it was described in the book.

Noh was a major inspiration for the novelist Mishima Yukio. Mishima's *Hōjō no umi* (*Sea of Fertility*) tetralogy draws extensively from noh; the title of the fourth book, *Tennin gosui* (*The Decay of the Angel*), is taken from a line in the play *Hagoromo*. The four novels follow the noh convention of the *waki* and *shite*, with narrator Honda Shigekuni serving as the *waki* throughout. The structure also calls to mind the five categories of noh plays, namely, *kami mono* (god plays), *shura mono* (warrior plays), *katsura mono* (woman plays), *kyōran mono* (madness plays), and *oni mono* (demon plays).

Mishima's *Eirei no koe* (Voices of the Heroic Dead) is another work that employs noh motifs. The souls of kamikaze pilots are summoned with a stone whistle—whose sound the noh flute is said to mimic—and called upon to tell their tale. And of course, Mishima is also known for his own updated versions of traditional noh pieces (translated as *Five Modern Noh Plays* by Donald Keene).

Works by contemporary novelists like Murakami Haruki and Nashiki Kaho are reminiscent of the *mugen* noh form developed by Zeami, where a human *waki* interacts with nonhuman characters. Noh provided fodder for such distinguished critics as Shirasu Masako. It also inspired the work of many manga artists, including Kai Yukiko and her sister Hatsu Akiko, Kihara Toshie, Yamagishi Ryōko, and Narita Minako. These works have spawned a new generation of noh fans. *Kurenai tennyo*, originally a fictional noh play depicted in the popular manga series *Garasu no kamen* (Glass Mask) by Miuchi Suzue, was made into an actual play, which was performed around the country to full houses. There are also numerous manga guides to noh plays.

The study of noh was once a privilege reserved for society's elites. After World War II, noh and *utai* spread rapidly as a hobby, as corporations sponsored noh clubs for their employees, and professional and semiprofessional teachers started giving lessons in the community. Unfortunately, corporate noh clubs are on the decline, and the population of amateur noh and *utai* devotees is shrinking. Nonetheless, I expect *utai* to stage another resurgence as people rediscover its value as a cultural anchor in these turbulent times.

CHAPTER IV

FORM AND FUNCTION

Five Categories of Plays

Of the roughly two thousand noh plays in existence, a little more than two hundred are regularly performed today, with the repertoire varying somewhat from one school to the next.[1] Most of these were written in the early part of the Muromachi period (1336–1573). Quite a few are of unknown authorship, but the best-known playwrights are Kan'ami, Zeami (Kan'ami's son), Kanze Motomasa (Zeami's son), Konparu Zenchiku (Zeami's son-in-law), Kanze Nobumitsu (the son of Zeami's nephew On'ami), and Konparu Zenpō (Zenchiku's grandson). Another noted playwright, Nobumitsu's son Kanze Nagatoshi, was active in the late Muromachi period. All embraced standard noh conventions, but each had his own distinctive style.

Fewer plays were written after the Tokugawa shogunate took ownership of noh in the Edo period (1603–1868). A number of new

---

1. Many of the plays outside the standard professional repertoire—including the previously mentioned *Akechi-uchi*, detailing Hideyoshi's military exploits—can be found in the fifty-three-volume *Mikan yōkyokushū* (Previously Unpublished Noh Plays), compiled by noh scholar and *kotsuzumi* performer Tanaka Makoto (stage name Hotaka Mitsuharu) and published by Koten Bunko from 1963 to 1998.

works appeared after the 1868 Meiji Restoration (many of them with martial themes), but they rarely endured past their premieres. The plays that form the bulk of the modern repertoire thus date from the Muromachi period.

Noh plays are grouped into five categories on the basis of their *shite* (protagonist) and theme. The first type of play, known as *kami mono* (or, alternatively, *waki* noh), revolves around a deity, or kami. This protagonist typically appears in disguise in the first act to narrate the history of a local spot of special religious or historical significance—a Shintō shrine, for example—and then returns in the second act in divine form to offer a blessing and perform an energetic dance.

The second type of play, *shura mono*, depicts a warrior, generally a character from the *Heike monogatari* (*Tale of the Heike*), whose ghost returns to tell the tale of his death in battle and ensuing torment in hell. The third is *katsura mono*, in which the leading character appears as an elegant woman. Many of noh's greatest masterpieces belong to this category, which is marked by subdued and graceful refinement. Such roles pose a special challenge for actors, as expressing depth despite the restrained movement requires great skill.

The fourth category is *kyōran mono*, depicting a character driven mad by the loss of a lover or child. This category is also a kind of grab bag for plays that do not fit into any other category; hence the alternate name *zatsu* noh (miscellaneous plays). *Oni mono*, the fifth category, comprises plays about demons, ghosts, water imps, strange beasts, and other supernatural beings.

There is one special play that falls into none of these categories: *Okina*. Unlike other plays, *Okina* has no plot. Attributed to the semi-legendary sixth-century figure Hata no Kawakatsu (see chapter 2), it is more in the nature of a prayer or ritual than a drama. The meaning of the text is a mystery. The Zen Buddhist monk Kawaguchi Ekai (1866–1945), the first recorded Japanese visitor to Tibet, wrote in the daily *Asahi Shimbun* that the opening lines—"tōtō tarari tarari ra"—were in fact Tibetan. The claim was immediately refuted, but when I asked about this during my own visit to Tibet, I was told that the words closely resembled an invocation at the beginning of the *Epic of King*

Gesar, a cycle performed widely in Tibet and Central Asia. Listening to it sung, I was struck by the similarity.

Zeami noted that noh is derived from *kagura* and other Shintō ceremonies. Like the Gesar cycle, *Okina* is performed to invoke the gods, and it retains a strong sense of the sacred. In the past, it would have opened a noh program that lasted an entire day, presenting plays in each of the five categories interspersed with *kyōgen* comedy. Such marathon performances have become rare in this day and age. But an awareness of the context and order in which different plays were originally performed can add greatly to our appreciation.

The Mystique of the Mask

It is impossible to discuss noh without mentioning the masks, one of the form's defining features. On this subject, however, I must rely heavily on what I have learned from *shite* colleagues and mask carvers, since—as a *waki* actor—I myself do not wear a mask on stage.

The Japanese have raised the art of mask making to levels seldom seen elsewhere in the world. Whether we are speaking of masks for noh, *kagura*, or *gagaku* (ancient music of the imperial court), the variety and attention to detail are extraordinary.

Noh masks are also remarkably expressive when used properly. A single mask can convey deep sadness or bliss, depending on the angle of the head. The actor's subtlest movement and even his state of mind can alter the effect. The secret to this expressive adaptability, according to one mask carver, lies in the exquisitely modeled contours of the eyelids and the area under the eyes.

The mask by itself, of course, is static and emotionally neutral; in fact, in Japanese, expressionless faces are commonly compared to noh masks. But it is this very neutrality that permits the expression of such a wide range of emotions. When viewed by itself, as an artwork, the mask is mute, no matter how finely crafted. But when worn by a seasoned actor, it can speak volumes. This is when the mask, also called the *omote* (face or surface), takes over as the face of the actor. In the handful of plays where the *shite* wears no mask, the actual face of the actor becomes the *omote* and—like the wooden variety—displays no overt expression.

Noh scholar Masuda Shōzō has written that when an actor puts on an *omote*, it becomes his real face. Again, it may seem paradoxical, but by covering his face with a mask, he heightens the emotion instead of suppressing it. After all, our facial expressions do a good job of hiding our true feelings. The mask, by concealing that surface display, opens the way for a deeper and truer expression of feeling. This also helps explain why male actors can portray feminine characters so convincingly.

Aesthetically, the use of masks dovetails with other conventions and stylistic features of noh, such as the *suriashi* (sliding) style of moving across the stage and the stiff, angular costumes. Masuda observes that noh's very lack of realism is what makes it timeless and universal. The *shite* of a noh drama—whether human or divine—embodies the essence of certain universal human passions or sentiments. A realistic depiction would reduce that essence to something specific to a particular time, place, and individual. Realism is rooted in a specific temporal context and as a result quickly becomes dated. This is why movies and TV dramas produced even a couple of decades ago so often strike one as old-fashioned. With the *mugen* noh form, Zeami freed drama from the constraints of space and time by avoiding the direct depiction of human emotion and experience. In this way, the very features of noh that might appear to limit its expression—including its masks—have instead expanded its range and earned it international acclaim.

For the actor, the noh mask is also an aid to mystical metamorphosis. Tied tightly to the actor's head, the mask has only tiny openings for the eyes, severely restricting the performer's field of vision. (At workshops for the general public, participants who put on masks are always surprised at how little they can see and how dark everything becomes.) Not being able to see much of their surroundings, actors naturally turn their attention inward. Openings for the mouth, too, are either very small or nonexistent, so that actors wind up inhaling their own breath and running low on oxygen. Meanwhile, they must dance. These are ideal conditions for a mental state resembling a trance. In this state, actors must be guided by intuition and, in essence, allow themselves to be inhabited by the nonhuman characters they are portraying. (Similar techniques are used to induce a trance suggesting divine possession in traditional *kagura* dances.)

Noh Songs—A Lost Lingua Franca

Until relatively recently, the influence of noh was felt throughout Japanese society. It was disseminated above all through the medium of *utai*, sung passages from famous noh plays. From the Edo period on, it was customary for people of all walks to sing the appropriate *utai* at various celebratory events. Many of these songs, taken from such auspicious plays as *Takasago*, *Shōjō*, and *Tamanoi*, were taught at the *terakoya* temple schools established for commoners in the Edo period. Knowledge of *utai* was also disseminated through the publication of *utaibon*, the noh equivalents of libretti. With the rise of commercial publishing in the Edo period, such books became extremely popular.[2] A shared knowledge of *utai* fostered fellowship and a sense of community.

At weddings, guests typically sang multiple excerpts from *Takasago*, a famous play celebrating the relationship of a long-married, devoted couple.[3] Other *utai* were sung to celebrate a youth's coming of age or the completion of a zodiac cycle on one's sixtieth birthday. People well-versed in *utai* often served as the masters of ceremonies at such events. The custom persisted in many parts of Japan until a few decades ago, and it still endures in some communities.

Until twenty or thirty years ago, weddings in the community of Tajiri in Miyagi prefecture were filled with *utai* from start to finish. First the groom's party would visit the bride's home and sing. Then

---

2. Three publishers continue to issue *utaibon* today: Hinoki Shoten (for the Kanze and Kongō schools), Wan'ya Shoten (Hōshō and Konparu schools), and Nōgaku Shorin (Kita school, along with an earlier edition of the Kanze school *utaibon* and those used by the Umewaka group). They also publish a variety of books on the subject of noh.

3. The best-known *utai* from *Takasago* (often sung during wedding scenes in period dramas) is that which begins, "Takasago ya, kono urabune ni, ho o agete" (At Takasago, we hoist the sail on this small boat).

Photo courtesy of Toyoma Co., Ltd.

The townspeople in the Toyoma district of Miyagi prefecture were so enamored of noh that local donors financed the construction of a noh stage in 1996, designed by renowned architect Kuma Kengo. It is a beautiful and largely open-air stage befitting its name—Mori Butai Noh Theater, or "Noh Stage in the Forest."

everyone would go to the groom's home and sing again at the sound of a bell. Throughout the ceremony, the guests would sing prescribed pieces. There were even songs about amorous encounters to counsel the embarrassed couple on what was supposed to happen on their wedding night. After food and drinks were served, the bride's party would sing their adieus, the groom's side would answer with an entreaty to stay a while longer, and so forth. The ceremony did not come to an end until late at night, when all joined together to sing *senshūraku*, the closing passage of *Takasago*, with its blessings for "a thousand autumns."

The Nagano town of Obuse (known as a haunt of the ukiyo-e artist Katsushika Hokusai) retains an old sake-drinking custom in which one drinker sings an *utai* while pouring for the other, and the recipient offers a song in return. The practice was relatively common until the 1960s and 1970s but is now rarely encountered outside of Obuse.

(Incidentally, the Hōshō school *shite* actor Sano Noboru is very active in Obuse, where he has been working to preserve such traditions while teaching noh to area children.)

My point is that, for much of our history, noh was not simply a spectacle to be observed but an integral element of Japanese culture and society at almost every level. Even those who never attended a play or took a noh lesson participated actively through the singing of *utai*. This kind of literacy has become rare (although older audience members may sometimes be seen following along with their own *utaibon*). The writer and rap artist Itō Seikō—an apprentice of mine—has lamented the sharp distinction between performer and listener that has emerged in modern times. Unfortunately, noh has not escaped this dualism.

Incidentally, knowledge of *utai* served another important purpose back in premodern times. The literary style in which the text was written (distinguished by the copula *sōrō*) served as a lingua franca for samurai living in different parts of the country with mutually unintelligible dialects. When the warrior elite from far-flung domains assembled at the shōgun's castle, the language of *utai* provided a standard dialect that everyone could understand. The distinctive literary style of noh texts continued to be used in the Meiji era, as seen in the letters of the great novelist Natsume Sōseki.

Samurai and *Suriashi*

Noh performers practice a distinctive manner of moving around the stage without lifting their heels from the floor. Called *suriashi*, this method of propulsion, with the pelvis kept parallel to the ground, makes full use of the core muscles, especially the psoas major. For the samurai of the Edo period, who were required to wear two heavy and cumbersome swords in public, *suriashi* was a means of moving about swiftly and smoothly while minimizing stress on the lower back. Noh thus incorporated a form of movement uniquely suited to the samurai, who were routinely schooled in the art.

The samurai of the Edo period were military men, and they were also the country's rulers and administrators. They embraced learning and the arts as marks of their elite status. After the Meiji Restoration, men in uniform were no longer encouraged to acquire such cultural refinements. I have never heard of cadets being taught *utai* or *waka* poetry at prewar military schools.

Paradoxically, it was under the military rule of the Tokugawa shogunate that Japan enjoyed more than 250 years of uninterrupted peace. Lasting peace—after the unceasing conflict that had plagued Japan since the middle of the fifteenth century—was the overarching goal pursued by Tokugawa Ieyasu as founder of the shogunate. This same desire for peace may help explain the subsequent decision to elevate noh to the status of *shikigaku*, the official dance and music of the shogunate.

Maintaining peace requires more than a decree from the top. All human beings are capable of violence, and warriors make a profession of it. The Tokugawa shogunate's adoption of noh as an institution may well have been an attempt to redirect the energies of the samurai from warfare to dance—which has deep and ancient links to the martial arts. The development of the noh repertoire backs up this interpretation. At the beginning of the Edo period, it still featured many swordfighting plays called *kirikumi* noh. But following noh's designation as *shikigaku*, outward displays of violence receded, and the emphasis shifted to a restrained, internalized mode of expression. This was an ingenious and effective means of sublimating the volatile energy of the military into peaceful pursuits—a strategy no doubt informed by Ieyasu's own firsthand experience of noh's efficacy.

The Genius of *Jo-Ha-Kyū*

One of the basic compositional principles put forth in Zeami's three-part treatise *Nōsakusho* (The Book of Noh Composition; also known as the *Sando*, or Three Elements) is the concept of *jo-ha-kyū*. Roughly translated as "opening-development-climax," *jo-ha-kyū* has applications that extend far beyond noh. In fact, I use it all the time, not only when working on a new theatrical production but also when composing a letter, writing an article, or preparing a lecture.

In noh, *jo* functions to draw the audience into the story, setting the stage while using clues and other devices to foreshadow the development ahead. *Ha* is the substance of the story, where the particulars are spelled out. This is the part where people in the audience are most apt to nod off. (And, in fact, the *ha* section may be deliberately designed to induce a dreamlike state and tap into the subconscious.) With the arrival of the *kyū* portion, however, the pace of the play picks up and everyone in the theater becomes wide-eyed with anticipation.

In a typical noh play, *jo* corresponds to the entrance and soliloquy of the *waki*, which sets the scene for what follows. *Ha* is the part when the *shite*—in the guise of a human—appears and narrates a tale. And *kyū* is the climactic second act, when the transformed *shite* reappears and (most often) performs a dance to close the play.

The *jo*, *ha*, and *kyū* phases of a play can each be further subdivided into their own *jo*, *ha*, and *kyū* portions. In the play's core *ha* section, for example, the *shite*'s slow entrance is *jo*; the dialogue between the *shite* and *waki* is *ha*; and *kyū* is the hurried exit of the *shite* upon the revelation of its true identity.

In his 1977 *Ongaku no kongen ni aru mono* (The Origins of Music), ethnomusicologist Koizumi Fumio (1927–83) wrote that while the original concept of *jo-ha-kyū* may have come from India or the Korean Peninsula, Zeami gave it new meaning, using it to guide not only shifts in tempo but also modes of expression. He elevated it to an aesthetic principle that could be applied to everything from music and theater to flower arrangement, tea ceremony, calligraphy, martial arts, and literature. Koizumi also pointed out that *jo-ha-kyū* as it evolved in Japan consists not of three distinct parts but of organically interrelated elements, each of which contains the other two. In *jo* lie the seeds of *ha*; *kyū* anticipates the ensuing *jo*. (The same phenomenon, he noted, can be observed in the martial arts, where the first few moves of a contest contain all the essential elements of what will follow.)

The *jo-ha-kyū* pattern can be discerned even today in a typical TV samurai drama. Let us say the story concerns a poor but honest man who falls victims to evildoers. The early section that introduces us to the victim and his plight corresponds to *jo*. The *ha* portion is when we see him tricked and victimized by the villains. In the *kyū*—typically about three-quarters of the way through—the hero and his band arrive and defeat the rogues in a sword fight, and justice is done. When an episode does not follow this pattern, viewers are left feeling dissatisfied.

The *jo-ha-kyū* structure can also be seen in mythology and folklore from around the world—which may help account for noh's universal appeal. The American scholar Joseph Campbell discusses this basic structure in his analysis of the "monomyth," or "hero's journey" narrative. American film director George Lucas was heavily influenced by Campbell and used the concept as a framework for his *Star Wars* movies.

The main difference between Campbell's monomyth and Zeami's noh is that the former emphasizes concrete, outward change, as the hero triumphs over the enemy and returns home transformed, with the power to rescue or renew his community. In noh, by contrast, no physical change takes place; the transformation is purely internal. The protagonist merely tells a story—occasionally a spiteful one—and disappears. The *shite* finds salvation through this exchange with the *waki*. The *waki*, representing the living, is also changed by the encounter, which transforms his (and our) perception of reality. It is a different path to renewal.

The Noh Stage

First-time visitors to a noh theater are often surprised to see a roof suspended over the stage. As I explained in chapter 3, noh was performed outdoors up through the Edo period, and the indoor theaters built in the Meiji era retained the traditional design. But the transition to the modern era was not entirely seamless.

Until the advent of electricity in the late nineteenth century, noh performances were illuminated only by natural light or by the dim, flickering light of candles, lanterns, and occasionally torches. Apparently the use of electric lighting in the Meiji era touched off considerable debate. As late as 1933, Tanizaki Jun'ichirō argued, in his essay *In'ei raisan* (*In Praise of Shadows*), that the noh stage should be left dark to preserve its mysterious beauty. Perhaps this preference is natural, given the religious and ceremonial roots of noh. Even today, when modern lighting is taken for granted, some complain that noh theaters are too bright.

Firelight noh at Kōfuku-ji temple in Nara has a long and illustrious history, but it was suspended for much of the late nineteenth and early twentieth century. Tradition has it that on the occasion of the custom's revival, with the famed noh scholar Nogami Toyoichirō (1883–1950) in the audience, an electric lamp was hung in a tree to supplement the traditional lighting. Nogami found the effect so incongruous that he climbed the tree and removed it.[4]

But let us return to the noh stage itself. Another vestige from the days when outdoor performances were the rule is the *shirasu*, the border of white pebbles around the stage. The *kizahashi*, a small staircase at the front of the stage (generally consisting of three steps), was formerly used by temple and shrine officials to announce the start of a performance, and by actors to receive gifts from the shōgun or daimyō.

The *hashigakari* is a passageway leading diagonally back from the stage. In Zeami's day, the corridor led straight back, but over time the angle has changed, and the passage has come to function as a performance space where important scenes take place. The *hashigakari* at the National Noh Theatre in Tokyo is set at a sharper angle than most, with the result that some musicians complain they find it difficult to tell when an actor has entered.

An interesting, if inconspicuous, feature of most noh stages is the placement of large clay jars beneath the floorboards to amplify the voices and the stamping of the feet. (The National Noh Theatre, which is relatively new, uses other mechanisms to enhance volume and resonance.)

Another contrivance that may not be obvious at first glance is the orientation of the floorboards, which run parallel to the front

---

4. Nogami was a scholar of English literature as well as noh, and he served as president of Hōsei University, which is home to the Nogami Memorial Noh Theatre Research Institute.

of the stage toward the rear and perpendicular near the front. This helps mask-wearing actors feel their way to the correct spot on stage with their feet. The aptly named *metsuke-bashira* (eye-fixing pillar) is another way that actors position themselves on stage.

The rear wall, called the *kagami-ita*, is always painted with the image of an aged pine, said to be based on the sacred Yōgō pine tree at Kasuga Grand Shrine in Nara, where early noh was performed. More generally, the evergreen pine is associated with immortality and regarded as an auspicious symbol.

The Noh Stage

Source: Illustration reprinted and text translated from *Manga de tanoshimu 'nō kyōgen* (Enjoying Noh ard Kyōgen through Manga), Hinoki Shoten, 1996.

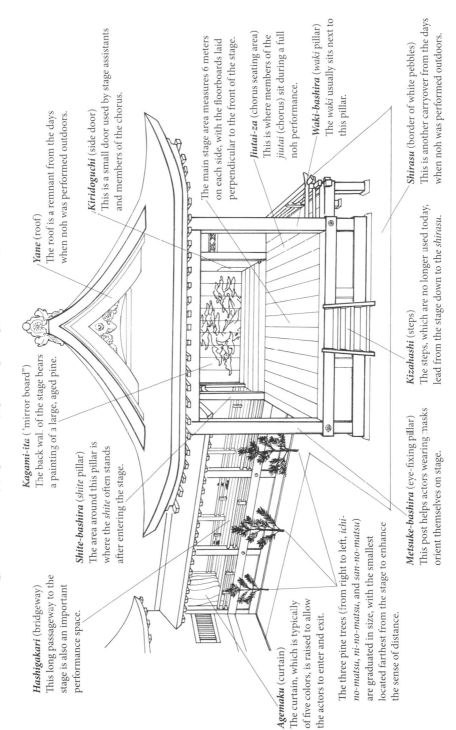

Hashigakari (bridgeway)
This long passageway to the stage is also an important performance space.

Agemaku (curtain)
The curtain, which is typically of five colors, is raised to allow the actors to enter and exit.

The three pine trees (from right to left, *ichi-no-matsu*, *ni-no-matsu*, and *san-no-matsu*) are graduated in size, with the smallest located farthest from the stage to enhance the sense of distance.

Metsuke-bashira (eye-fixing pillar)
This post helps actors wearing masks orient themselves on stage.

Kagami-ita ("mirror board")
The back wal of the stage bears a painting of a large, aged pine.

Shite-bashira (*shite* pillar)
The area around this pillar is where the *shite* often stands after entering the stage.

Yane (roof)
The roof is a remnant from the days when noh was performed outdoors.

Kiridoguchi (side door)
This is a small door used by stage assistants and members of the chorus.

The main stage area measures 6 meters on each side, with the floorboards laid perpendicular to the front of the stage.

Jiutai-za (chorus seating area)
This is where members of the *jiutai* (chorus) sit during a full noh performance.

Waki-bashira (*waki* pillar)
The *waki* usually sits next to this pillar.

Shirasu (border of white pebbles)
This is another carryover from the days when noh was performed outdoors.

Kizahashi (steps)
The steps, which are no longer used today, lead from the stage down to the *shirasu*.

CHAPTER V

THE GENIUS OF ZEAMI

Zeami Motokiyo (1363–c. 1443) is best known for the development of the *mugen* noh form, his own oeuvre of outstanding plays, and his twenty-odd treatises on the performing arts. I have already introduced some of Zeami's achievements, but here I would like to devote an entire chapter to his genius and his legacy.

A Gift to the Shōgun

The young shōgun Ashikaga Yoshimitsu (r. 1368–94) took a great fancy to Zeami after seeing the twelve-year-old boy perform. At the Gion Festival three years later, Zeami served as a personal attendant to the country's most powerful man.

Such was the low social standing of professional actors at the time that the palace minister scolded Yoshimitsu for associating with "beggars." Unfazed by such insults, Zeami went on to elevate the social status of the performing arts in Japan.

Under the tutelage of top court official Nijō Yoshimoto, Zeami was schooled in *waka* (Japanese classical poetry), as well as the traditions, rules, and etiquette of courtly life. This was doubtless exactly what his father Kan'ami had in mind when he offered his son as a "gift" to the shōgun. Zeami excelled at poetry and courtly pastimes like *kemari* (a genteel form of football). He became familiar with Chinese poetry and such Chinese classics as the *Analects* of Confucius and *I Ching*, and he quoted from these works (though not always accurately) in his treatises on the performing arts. Zeami also incorporated his broad learning into his plays, creating a theatrical form that appealed to society's elite. He and his father Kan'ami introduced many innovations that steered their Kanze-za troupe toward the aesthetic refinement that distinguishes noh as a theatrical form.

Dream Noh

The *mugen* noh form perfected by Zeami, introduced in chapter 1, allows the deceased to give voice to feelings that were left unsaid in life and to reenact deeds that continue to torment them. Having recounted their tales, these protagonists, or *shite*, return to the abode of the dead with their burden lightened.

It is worth noting here that the foundations of *mugen* noh were probably laid long before Zeami appeared on the scene. The plot of *Aoi no ue* differs little from the chapter in *Genji monogatari* (*Tale of Genji*) concerning the torment inflicted on Lady Aoi by the spirit of a jealous rival. Such early antecedents suggest that Japanese audiences were already quite comfortable with narratives centering on the suffering of angry or grieving spirits and the solace they eventually find through the prayers of Buddhist priests. This was the scaffolding on which Zeami built the theatrical genre of *mugen* noh, which honors the departed by assigning the *waki* (and by extension, the audience) the task of listening to the spirits of the dead and sharing in their grief.

Thanks in large part to Zeami, Japanese theater reached a pinnacle of artistic maturity during the Muromachi period. In the West (perhaps with the exception of ancient Greece), the dramatic arts would not begin to gain similar social status until the appearance of William Shakespeare (1564–1616). (Only in modern times has it become commonplace for Shakespearean actors to be graduates of top British universities like Oxford and Cambridge or to be conferred knighthoods.)

Donald Keene has expounded at length on noh's literary depth and complexity, while also stressing the subtlety and ambiguity that allow readers and viewers to draw what they will from a work. As literature and dramatic art, Zeami's noh is no less an achievement than Shakespeare's work.

From Outcast to Hero

The myth of Yamasachihiko and Umisachihiko, discussed in chapter 2, relegated the performing arts to a subservient role. Actors were descended from clowns or jesters who demonstrated their submission to the powerful by inviting derision. But Zeami forged a different path. Instead of pandering to the audience, he turned theater into an art that set its own standards.

I once had an opportunity to lead a workshop for *hikikomori*, shut-ins who have withdrawn from social life for psychological reasons. Each participant was asked to give a presentation, which was a big challenge for them, since they were unaccustomed to being with other people, let alone speaking in front of them.

Being exposed to the gaze of others makes us self-conscious. This, explains existential psychologist Rollo May (1909–94), can give rise to a sense of ourselves as "objects" devoid of autonomy, controlled by others and their expectations of us. Overcoming the tyranny of such expectations requires that we become "subjects" directed by our own feelings and wishes. For the participants in the workshop, the challenge was to transform themselves from passive objects of scrutiny to subjects actively transmitting their own message.

One might say that Zeami similarly sought to transform stage performers from lowly objects of derision into true "actors"—artists who set their own standards of excellence.

Through noh, Zeami transformed the outcast into a hero—both in real life and on the stage. What we see in noh, instead of the self-abasement of the vanquished, is the nobility of defeat. The protagonists of *mugen* noh are typically defeated heroes. The play *Tsuchigumo* ends with the slaying of a spider-like monster, but before that comes a spectacular fight scene in which the defiant beast shoots its web in all directions to foil its assailants—generally to enthusiastic applause from the audience.

Kyōgen, noh's comedic sibling, turns the tables in its own way. *Kyōgen* and noh were born around the same time and evolved together. While noh is centered on song and dance, *kyōgen* consists primarily of dialogue and clearly harks back to the court-jester origins of the performing arts. Nonetheless, *kyōgen* ridiculed those in power by depicting lords as egotistical simpletons outwitted by their lackeys. (The daimyō of premodern times had the magnanimity to laugh when they saw themselves portrayed as the butt of such pranks, but it seems that Meiji leaders were more easily offended.)

In addition to ridiculing the elite by having servants get the better of their masters, *kyōgen* took jabs at noh itself by parodying famous pieces in the repertoire. An example is the *kyōgen* play *Fukuro yamabushi* (The Owl and the Mountain Ascetic), a spoof of *Aoi no ue* (Lady Aoi). Both plays feature a *yamabushi*—a mountain ascetic with supernatural powers—who is summoned to exorcise an evil spirit. In *Aoi no ue*, the ascetic invokes the power of Buddhist deities to quell Lady Rokujō's jealous fury against her lover's wife and awakens in her the divine compassion of a bodhisattva. In *Fukuro yamabushi*, the ascetic is summoned to drive away the spirit of an owl that has taken possession of the younger of two brothers. Unfortunately, the priest's prayers only make things worse, and soon the older brother is behaving like an owl, too. Undaunted, the *yamabushi* perseveres. He is about to give up, though, and leave the stage, when he, too, begins to hoot.

The Dream Pavilion

One of the means by which Zeami and his contemporaries elevated their position was to redesign the stage. The Japanese word for theater, *shibai*, literally means "on the lawn." In other words, the stage may originally have been on low ground, with the audience "looking down" on the performance. Zeami made qualitative changes to the plain, simple stage conventionally used by *sarugaku* troupes, raising it above the audience and covering it with a roof supported by pillars. The pillars, while maintaining the openness of the performing area, framed the stage in a way that called to mind the *himorogi*, a Shintō worship space with a sacred evergreen *sakaki* in the center. On such a stage, the actors were more akin to deities conferring blessings on the audience than jesters performing at the whim of their superiors. To many, the noh stage still exudes an aura of sanctity.

Educational psychologist Manita Akira once told me that he considered the *hashigakari*—the passageway leading to the stage—analogous to the birth canal. Manita was well versed in noh and even made Zeami's *Fūshikaden* required reading for his graduate-level courses in clinical psychology. He likened the *kagami-no-ma* just beyond the curtain to the womb and the main stage to the world into which we are born. The actor's slow, deliberate entrance onto the stage via the narrow *hashigakari*, he said, symbolizes the painful process of being born into this world.

The actors' exit at the end of the play is just as mysterious. After the chorus and musicians finish, there is a moment of silence as they place their fans and instruments on the floor—a pause that allows the viewers to reorient themselves, as if awakening from a dream. The actors then move quietly and deliberately offstage, the same way they entered. At this point, some in the audience may applaud, but others simply let out a long breath. (Applause is not obligatory at a noh performance, as it is in the West, nor is a big, long round of applause necessarily the most appropriate expression of appreciation. There are no curtain calls because there is no drop curtain—only an *agemaku* at the end of the *hashigakari*, lifted by stage attendants with bamboo poles.)

Another interesting analysis of the noh stage is that offered by French playwright, poet, and diplomat Paul Claudel (1868–1955), who immersed himself in Japanese culture during his years as ambassador to Japan, from 1921 to 1927. In his 1926 essay "Nō," he described the noh stage as the "pavilion of the dream," protruding into a sea of spectators. He also commented that a noh play unfolds in the mind of the viewer, as well as on the stage. By that, I think, he meant not merely that the viewer's imagination is an active participant but also that noh can lead the mind inward even as it draws the eye outward, awakening insights and taking the viewer on a spiritual journey. The noh stage is perfectly designed for such an experience.

Noh's International Reach

Thanks to people like Claudel, noh has made its influence felt far beyond Japan's shores, particularly in France. Its impact on Claudel's own literary work is evident, for example, in the 1935 oratorio *Jeanne d'Arc au bûcher (Joan of Arc at the Stake)*. The drama itself consists largely of flashbacks that Joan experiences while chained to the stake awaiting execution. She is visited and comforted by Saint Dominic, founder of the Dominican order, before she ascends to heaven. From Claudel's use of a chorus and the combination of sung and spoken lines, it is clear that he based his libretto on the *mugen* noh form, casting Joan as the *shite* and Dominic as the *waki*. Claudel's work was adapted for the noh stage by Kanō Shūhō, a Kita school actor. Simply titled *Jeanne d'Arc*, it was performed in May 2012 at the Jeanne d'Arc International Festival in France.

Claudel was by no means the only Western artist on whom noh left a deep and lasting impression. German architect Bruno Taut praised the expressive minimalism of noh and the noh stage. Benjamin Britten's 1964 opera *Curlew River* was inspired by the noh play *Sumidagawa*, about a grief-stricken mother on a journey in search of her kidnapped son. William Butler Yeats incorporated features of noh in his 1916 one-act play *At the Hawk's Well* about Cú Chulainn, the mythological hero of ancient Ulster. This work, in turn, was adapted for noh as *Takahime* (Hawk Princess), which has been performed many times over the years. (One critically acclaimed international production featured Umewaka Genshō, a living national treasure, and the Irish choral ensemble Anúna.)

Richard Emmert, an American-born professor of Asian performance at Musashino University in Tokyo, is the founder and artistic director of Theatre Nohgaku, a troupe performing noh in English. Emmert has produced his own adaptation of Yeats's *At the Hawk's*

Well, with himself in the leading role. New noh plays continue to be written and performed in English, expanding noh's reach inside and outside of Japan.

Ensuring Continuity

Let us return now to Zeami's achievements. In addition to perfecting noh as an art form, he ensured its establishment and survival as a tradition by institutionalizing the transmission of skills from generation to generation, instead of trusting to the genius or commitment of particular individuals. One important means to this end was the establishment of a hereditary *iemoto* system, in which the leadership of a school is passed down in a straight line from the founder to the successive male heads of the *ie*—the family or household.

Technically, it was Kan'ami who got the ball rolling when he passed the leadership of his troupe to his son Zeami. This sort of patrilineal transmission had long existed in Japan, but it was quite unusual in the performing arts prior to Kan'ami. Zeami, too, was determined to preserve the tradition by passing it down in a single unbroken line. Having no male issue for many years, he initially named his adopted son as heir, but he revoked the decision after the birth of a natural son, Motomasa. The system that Kan'ami initiated and Zeami institutionalized is alive and well today in the five traditional schools of noh, each of which traces its lineage directly back to its founder.

The *iemoto* system has been criticized for prioritizing lineage over individual merit, but if the ultimate goal is continuity, there is no better system. Merit-based succession opens the door to endless internal disputes that can weaken, splinter, and even destroy an organization, especially during times of social upheaval. Zeami embraced the *iemoto* system in the belief that it could withstand such vicissitudes, and it is owing to that framework that noh has endured for six and a half centuries.

Moreover, Zeami made it clear that blood kinship was not the determining factor in succession; an heir could easily be adopted into the family where appropriate. In fact, in Zeami's view, one became part of the *ie* (household) by embracing the family tradition, not the other way around. Continuity comes before pedigree. The *iemoto* system may not be perfect, but from the standpoint of organizational governance (including business management), it deserves a second look.

Balance through Orchestration

Zeami also contributed immeasurably to noh's long-term survival and success by codifying various principles and dictums to guide the artists. One of his most basic precepts was to seek balance between the forces of yin and yang. "Any endeavor will meet with success at the point when the principles of yin and yang are harmonized," he wrote.[1] He went on to explain the need for an actor to perform in a more restrained manner (yin) on sunny days, when the audience was in high spirits (yang), and, conversely, with greater power and exuberance on cloudy or rainy days, when the crowd tended to be subdued.

But adjusting one's performance to the audience's mood is easier said than done, as every stand-up comedian knows. A cold, unresponsive audience can throw a performer off, and the harder you try, the icier the reaction gets. Countering the audience's yin with too much yang is likely to backfire. Fortunately, noh actors have the support of the *hayashi* accompanists (actually, artists and co-creators in their own right), whose instruments combine to achieve the optimum balance—even self-adjusting to the weather.

The *hayashi* consists of four instruments: *fue* (flute), *kotsuzumi* (shoulder drum), *ōtsuzumi* (hip drum), and *taiko* (stick drum). The two hand-held drums—*kotsuzumi* and *ōtsuzumi*—have contrasting roles and traits. The former requires moisture and sounds best in humid weather; in fact, during a performance, players will sometimes apply saliva to a piece of *washi* paper on the drum's skin to maintain the instrument's tone. As a rule, the *kotsuzumi* is struck on the second and fourth beats. Accentuation of the "upbeat," as in jazz or rock, tends to speed up the tempo.

---

1. Translated by J. Thomas Rimer in Yamazaki Masakazu, ed., *On the Art of the Nō Drama*, Princeton University Press, 1984, p. 20.

The *ōtsuzumi*, by contrast, is at its best when the weather is dry. The skins of these drums are dried in front of a brazier before each performance. The *ōtsuzumi* is usually sounded on the first and third beats, and when these beats are dominant, the tempo tends to slow down.

In other words, on cloudy or dank days, the *kotsuzumi* dominates, and the pace picks up; on clear, crisp days, the *ōtsuzumi* dominates, and the tempo eases. By their very nature, the instruments promote the balance of yin and yang that Zeami sought, without any conscious effort on the part of the performers.

No single person has been credited with this innovation; I suspect that it evolved over time. Still, the juxtaposition of instruments that complement one another in this fashion, automatically balancing the forces of yin and yang, counts among noh's more ingenious devices. By enabling professionals at any rank—not just virtuosos or geniuses like Zeami—to turn in compelling performances, it has surely contributed to noh's longevity.

Playing to the Audience

As the subtitle of this book indicates, noh is Japan's oldest theatrical tradition, having survived some 650 years. While its practitioners are grouped into schools that do not perform together, we know each other fairly well, and all of us share a desire to connect with as broad an audience as possible—not just noh aficionados but also those with little or no background. I see this as a legacy of Zeami's insistence that noh have universal appeal. "The greatest good fortune for the development of any troupe," he wrote," "is to bring happiness and earn the respect of their audiences."[2] Not content to win the acclaim of the learned, Zeami strove for a theatrical experience that could be enjoyed by all.

This orientation is reflected in the thematic diversity of Zeami's plays and also in his advice on acting. "When one thinks over the real purposes of our art," he wrote, "a player who truly can bring happiness to his audiences is one who can without censure bring his art to all, from the nobility to audiences in . . . the far-off provinces and

2. Ibid., p. 41

the various shrine festivals."[3] A true master, in his view, was an actor with the skill to captivate even those with no special knowledge of or interest in noh.

Zeami acknowledges that this is no easy feat but urges the beginner to think of it as an ideal to strive for. I believe that Zeami's emphasis on winning the love and respect of diverse audiences is both a key to noh's longevity and a condition for one's continued growth as an actor.

The Spirit of Mindful Detachment

Of the artistic principles Zeami introduced in his treatises, one of the best known is *riken no ken*, a detached view of oneself. (A related concept is *kensho dōshin no ken*, which can be translated as "the audience's perspective.") The idea is to envision oneself on the stage from different angles simultaneously—a challenge as confounding as a Zen kōan. In fact, the concept of *riken no ken* has its roots in the Buddhist idea of detached mindfulness, and it extends beyond performance to the way we view and interact with the world around us.

The *ami* of Kan'ami and Zeami is a Buddhist affix used by adherents of the Jishū sect of Pure Land Buddhism. Zeami saw noh not just as a form of entertainment but also as a kind of spiritual training by which, through tireless effort, the practitioner might achieve a state of mind akin to satori, or enlightenment.

In a sense, Zeami's Buddhist emphasis on spiritual detachment was a reflection of the uncertain times in which he lived. It was an era of warfare, famine, and successive natural calamities, when death was always near at hand. Although perpetual warfare gave way to peace in the Edo period, the uncertainty and transience of this life remained a given—not least for members of the warrior class, who could be ordered to commit seppuku (ritual suicide) at any time. Modern society makes it much easier for us to ignore death and banish thoughts of life's impermanence, yet we are still tormented by angst

---

3. Ibid.

and uncertainty. For professionals and amateurs alike, the practice of noh can be a haven of mindful non-attachment in these anxious times.

The noh actor's cultivation of *riken no ken* has a physiological side to it as well. Mirrors are not normally used in noh practice; instead, practitioners are trained to "see" themselves through proprioception. Neurons called proprioceptors, located within the muscles, tendons, and joints, allow human beings to sense their posture and the positions of their limbs and hands without the aid of sight. These sensors help us to stand upright, walk correctly, and keep our balance. But their function declines as we age, and this is one reason elderly people are apt to trip and fall. When I look around me and see all the noh performers who remain active and mobile despite their advanced age, it confirms my belief in noh training as a prescription for healthy longevity.

Pearls of Wisdom

Zeami left behind many memorable sayings and adages—not just clever or eloquent turns of phrase but deep and novel insights about the performing arts. Here is a small but representative selection.

Ups and Downs

Odoki and *medoki*, literally translated as "male time" and "female time," refer to the two phases of a yang-yin cycle. *Odoki* is the powerful phase, when everything goes our way. We feel upbeat and healthy, and luck seems to be on our side. Other people behave exactly as we want them to, as if anticipating our wishes. *Odoki* is when life is good. But then there are *medoki*, times when nothing seems to turn out right. We make unforced errors, our well-meaning statements are misconstrued and criticized, our body aches, and we just feel rotten.

Zeami was particularly concerned about coping with *medoki*. In his day, different noh troupes competed against one another at events called *tachiai*. Zeami advised his actors that when such contests fell on a *medoki*, they should be as restrained as possible in their performance, saving their efforts for the next *odoki* surge.

A *medoki* may pass in a day, or it may linger for weeks, months, even years. Zeami teaches us that when things are not going your way, there is no point in getting hysterical; the best policy is just to wait it out.

Timing Is of the Essence

"Toki ni mochiyuru o mote hana to shirubeshi" is a bit tricky to translate. It centers on the core concept of *hana* (lit. flower), an ineffable quality of artistic presence and authority discussed at greater length below. The thrust of this particular quotation is that *hana* is not a fixed or absolute quality but a fluid one, changing according to time and circumstance.

Timing is a famously important factor in any undertaking. Indeed, the importance of observing the proper time and season for each endeavor is a universal theme. It figures prominently in the *I Ching*, which Zeami quotes frequently, and in the Bible, as when Jesus says, "My time has not yet come" (John 7:6). *Hana* becomes manifest when one's judgment and actions are optimally suited to the season and the situation at hand.

Dedication without Ambition

"Keiko wa tsuyokare, jōshiki wa nakare," roughly translated, means to study and practice as hard as you can but without seeking any personal reward from such effort. *Keiko*, the Japanese word for practice in the context of the arts, incorporates the idea of respect for tradition and the skills of our predecessors. In the context of noh, this means devotion to the *utai* (song) and *mai* (dance) passed down since Zeami's day, as well as to one's teacher, who embodies noh's tradition and skills.

The pitfall to be avoided during such training is *jōshiki*—translated variously but generally thought of as indicating ambition or arrogance—which can lead to unhealthy egotism, competition, and bitterness. Devotion to the craft for its own sake, without hope for personal gain, may be the purest form of *keiko*.

The Mystery of *Hana*

Hana (flower) is the word Zeami used to sum up the magnetism and stage presence of a truly accomplished performer. In *Fūshikaden*, Zeami explains the quality in terms of two adjectives, *omoshiroki* and *mezurashiki*. However, he was not using those words as they are used today (to mean "interesting," and "unusual," respectively).

Zeami described *omoshiroki* as a sudden sensation of brightness. An example of this usage can be found in *Ise monogatari* (*The Tale of Ise*), written during the Heian period (794–1185). The protagonist, wandering dejectedly through the province of Mikawa (now Aichi prefecture) after being banished from the capital of Kyoto, comes upon a profusion of irises blooming in the most *omoshiroki* way, and as he gazes at the blue-violet flowers, his gloom dissipates. An *omoshiroki* performance is one that elicits a similar response from the audience. It is brightening, uplifting.

Mezurashiki, too, means much more than mere novelty. After all, even the most astonishing theatrical devices will cease to impress an audience the second or third time around. For Zeami, *mezurashiki* referred to something that naturally attracted the eye and charmed the heart, delighting audiences afresh each time they encountered it.

But how does one attain such rare qualities? Zeami's answer, and one of his best-known sayings, is "hisureba hana": "In secrecy blooms the flower." Always keep your intentions hidden, he exhorts, to achieve the maximum effect.

The performing arts are a bit like the emperor's new clothes: the audience must be made to see something that is not there. Efforts to maximize the performance's immediate impact through furious action or vivid realism can be successful in the short run, but they soon grow stale. The audience becomes jaded and demands something more. So it is that silent films gave way to talkies and black-and-white to color, followed by 3D and virtual reality. There is no end to the public's appetite for newer, "realer," more superficially stimulating forms of entertainment.

Noh refuses to feed this addiction. Rather than pander to the audience, noh forces viewers to accept it on its own terms. It is often devoid of overt action, and the archaic, poetic language can be hard to follow. Instead of depicting the setting in vivid detail, it asks viewers to use their imagination to see the moon and the mountains and hear the crash of the waves. This mysterious, elusive beauty is the very essence of *hana*.

In teaching as in acting, less is often more, and concealment can lead to revelation. In his memoirs, *waki* master Hōshō Arata (1870–1944) relates an anecdote about his great-grandfather, Hōshō Shinnojō. While still young and taking lessons from his father Shinpachirō, Shinnojō was practicing to perform the play *Hachinoki* at Edo Castle. For the most part, the rehearsals went smoothly, but there was one crucial line that Shinnojō could not deliver to his father's satisfaction, no matter how often he practiced it.

Finally, on the day of the performance, as an anxious Shinnojō was leaving his house, a messenger ran up with a note from his father. It read, "Sing the line without exaggeration." Suddenly the scales fell from the young actor's eyes. The more he had practiced, the further he had strayed from the most natural delivery. The revelation might seem like a small one, but for Shinnojō, it had a profound and lasting impact. Of course, Shinnōjō's father could have offered that advice much earlier, but that would have robbed his son of the chance to explore all the dimensions of the line for himself. Such are the secrets of *hana*.

An Old Tree That Still Blossoms

Another Zeami saying is "Inochi ni wa owari ari, nō ni wa hate aru bekarazu," which can be translated simply, "Life is finite, art has no end." (In Zeami's day, noh was called *sarugaku*, so the *nō* in this axiom refers more generally to artistic attainment.)

Life eventually comes to an end, but for the noh actor, there is no finish line. One continues to push the limits and make new discoveries throughout one's career. This dovetails with the notion of *shoshin* (beginner's mind), a process of breaking with the past and creating oneself anew at each stage in life (see chapter 1).

A lifelong pursuit does not necessarily mean a strenuous level of activity in old age, however. In *Fūshikaden*, Zeami discusses the best mode of activity for each age group and comments that those over fifty may gain new insight by doing less. Older actors should cede the leading roles of popular plays to their younger colleagues and focus on quieter pieces that demand greater depth of expression. In this way the actor's *hana* can continue to unfold.

"An old tree that still blossoms" is how Zeami described his father's art in his declining years. The same metaphor was applied to Kita school actor Tomoeda Kikuo (1908–96) in the 1993 book *Oiki no hana* (The Flower of an Aged Tree) by essayist and art critic Shirasu Masako. There is a rare and subtle *hana* that blooms defiantly after the body and voice have grown frail. It is not something a younger actor can mimic. Many noh actors actually look forward to the day when they will be able to perform those quiet, subdued parts to which only an elderly artist can do justice.

But such maturity cannot be rushed. My own teacher often admonished me to be patient. "Don't expect to be considered a great actor until your time has come," he said. "Just keep giving it your all."

CHAPTER VI

NOH AND THE TAPESTRY OF
JAPANESE LITERATURE

In the preceding chapters, I have examined some of the qualities that have contributed to noh's enduring success. Now I would like to explore noh's influence on other genres of Japanese literature, with a focus on two of its giants: Natsume Sōseki and Matsuo Bashō.

Sōseki and *Utai*

I have mentioned the fact that Natsume Sōseki (1867 1916), one of Meiji Japan's greatest novelists, had a deep grasp of noh. In fact, Sōseki studied seriously with Hōshō Arata (1870–1944), the head of my own Shimogakari Hōshō school, though this is not widely known.

Quite a few members of Sōseki's circle studied noh, including the literary critic Komiya Toyotaka, the noh scholar Nogami Toyoichirō, the novelist Nogami Yaeko (Toyoichirō's wife), the philosopher Abe Yoshishige, and the haiku poets Masaoka Shiki and Takahama Kyoshi.

Sōseki is said to have loved *utai* so much that not a day went by that he did not practice it. He first studied *utai* for about six months during his four-year stint teaching English in Kumamoto, from 1896 on. In 1900, he left Japan for London on a two-year government scholarship, and on his return he became a professor of English literature at Tokyo Imperial University. Around 1906, shortly before leaving his teaching position and joining the daily *Asahi Shimbun*, Sōseki began looking for a noh teacher with whom he might study noh seriously.[1] He was first introduced to Matsumoto Kintarō, a *shite* actor and the uncle of novelist Izumi Kyōka. But he ultimately opted to study under the *waki* actor Hōshō Arata, most likely on the recommendation of the haiku poet Takahama Kyoshi (1874–1959). Kyoshi was a native of Matsuyama in Ehime prefecture, a city with strong connections to noh, particularly Shimogakari Hōshō. He had studied *utai* since his youth and performed in several noh plays as a *waki*.

Sōseki was forty years old when he began taking lessons with Hōshō Arata.[2] Apparently, the relationship was rocky at times. For example, Sōseki complained that the fee was too high.[3] (He paid five yen per month for two lessons a week, a rather hefty sum at a time when grade school teachers made just ten to thirteen yen a month.) Moreover, Arata frequently failed to show up at Sōseki's home on the appointed day. On at least one occasion, the novelist became so annoyed that he notified his teacher of his intention to quit. Two or three days later, though, Arata appeared at the front door as if nothing had happened, and they took up where they had left off. Sōseki was still studying with Arata in January 1916, the year he (the novelist) died of a stomach ulcer.

Sōseki had satirized *utai* in *Wagahai wa neko de aru* (1905, *I Am a Cat*) and *Botchan* (1906), but as his engagement with noh deepened, he began actively employing noh conventions and motifs, starting with *Kusamakura* (1906, *The Three-Cornered World*). The title itself—literally, "grass pillow"—is a poetic term occurring frequently in noh plays; it refers to the improvised sleeping arrangements of life on the road.

---

1. The reasons for his decision to hone his *utai* skills are humorously depicted in "Ganjitsu" (New Year's Day), found in the collection of personal vignettes published in 1910 as *Eijitsu shōhin* (*Spring Miscellany*).
2. Arata, who was thirty-seven at the time, would go on to become one of the most celebrated figures in noh by the time he was forty-five.
3. See Kuribayashi Teiichi, *Sōseki to yōkyoku* (Sōseki and Utai), Hinoki Shoten, 1951.

Kusamakura begins with a long passage in which the narrator—a painter—bemoans the conflicting demands and complications of human life. He has embarked on a journey in order to flee from such worldly entanglements, much like a *waki* in a noh play. Arriving at a hot-spring resort in the mountains, he meets a shopkeeper who reminds him of the old woman in the play *Takasago*. From her he first hears about Onami, the young, divorced innkeeper who becomes his hostess—someone, like a *shite*, shrouded in mystery. The narrator and Onami talk at length about her ex-husband, about the Russo-Japanese War, and also about Western art and culture. *Kusamakura* is a dreamlike tale with the structure and feel of a *mugen* noh play. A number of Sōseki's subsequent works, particularly *Yume jūya* (1908, *Ten Nights Dreaming*) and *Kōjin* (1912, *The Wayfarer*), are also heavily influenced by noh.

Ambivalence toward the West

One indication that *Kusamakura* was inspired by noh is the lack of plot development. In fact, the novel's narrator lets us know that he cares little about plot; when reading a book, he says, he flips through and peruses passages at random. This may be a jab at traditional Western storytelling (going back to Aristotle's *Poetics*, which ranked plot as the most important element of tragedy). As such, it hints at Sōseki's ambivalence toward Western thought and civilization, which so many of his Meiji compatriots had embraced uncritically.

To Sōseki, noh seems to have represented the antithesis of Western drama. Noh lends itself to the kind of piecemeal, almost random appreciation advocated by the narrator of *Kusamakura*. *Koutai* are melodious passages of noh plays that can be sung alone, like arias. Similarly, *shimai* and *maibayashi* are short dance excerpts performed along with the *jiutai* chorus, with or without instrumental accompaniment.

Haiku, likewise, may have served as an antidote to Western literature for Sōseki. That he was a fan can be gathered from the number of haiku poets with whom he associated. Haiku and *utai* were closely linked, as I explain below. (The poet Masaoka Shiki was a great *utai* enthusiast, and Sōseki's *utai* master Hōshō Arata studied haiku with Shiki.)

Interestingly, Sōseki was much less enamored of kabuki. He once surmised that it had been created by people of very low intellect but relatively high artistic sensibility to meet the demand for entertainment by similarly minded people.[4] Kabuki actively strives to seduce and impress the audience. Noh, as Sōseki realized, is quite different. "The pleasure we gain from a noh play," Sōseki writes in *Kusamakura*, "springs not from any skill at presenting the raw human feelings of the everyday world but from clothing feeling 'as it is' in layer upon layer of art, and in a kind of slowed serenity of deportment not to be found in the real world."[5]

The two years Sōseki spent in London were, in his own words, the most unpleasant of his life. He found the rationalistic individualism of the host country so disorienting that he suffered a nervous breakdown. His impulse to find a noh teacher upon his return to Japan may well have been driven by a hunch that studying *utai* could have a therapeutic effect. In this context, *Kusamakura* can be read as a deliberate attempt by Sōseki to disengage himself from the individualism of the Western writers who had once inspired him, foreshadowing the Zen-like philosophy that he developed toward the end of his life: *Sokuten kyoshi* (Live in accord with heaven, devoid of the self).

Wellsprings of Bashō's Inspiration

Another literary titan whose work drew heavily on noh was the poet Matsuo Bashō (1644–94). Bashō was born in the province of Iga (now in Mie prefecture), known for its fierce independence and ultimately futile resistance against the warlord Oda Nobunaga in the late sixteenth century. By Bashō's time the province had become part of the Tsu domain, and Iga natives faced high hurdles to advancement

---

4. From the 1909 essay "Meiji-za no shokan o Kyoshi-kun ni towarete," written in reply to a question from Takahama Kyoshi about a kabuki performance at the Meiji-za.
5. As translated by Meredith McKinney in *Kusamakura*, Penguin Books, 2008.

within the domain's ruling apparatus. Ultimately, Bashō abandoned the attempt and moved to Edo (modern-day Tokyo) to make a living as a haikai poet, outside the rigid four-class framework of Edo-period society.

The poetic form Bashō studied was haikai (*haikai no renga* in full), a genre of playful linked verse that emerged in the sixteenth century. Even before Bashō transformed and elevated it to high art, haikai often quoted lines from noh plays, although mostly with humorous intent. According to one of Bashō's students, knowledge of *utai* was as fundamental to

A painting of Bashō by Hozumi Tōtō (detail).

haikai as a familiarity with *Genji monogatari* (*Tale of Genji*) was to classical poetry.

For Bashō, however, *utai* was much more than a textbook or a source of literary allusions. He looked to it to guide his life, particularly in his later years.

Despite the fame and success he earned as a poet in Edo, Bashō was haunted by a feeling of emptiness. In the early 1680s, hoping to fill that void, he took to the road—not as a modern-day tourist might but in the role of a spiritual seeker, like the *waki* itinerant monks of noh. We can glean this intent from an inscription (believed to be by Bashō) on a painting by fellow poet Hozumi Tōtō in a private collection. It comprises two elements. One is his own haiku: "Tabibito to / waga na yobaren / hatsu shigure" (Let my name / be traveler / first rains). The other is a passage from the noh play *Umegae*, ending with an invitation from the *shite* to the "traveler" to take shelter from the rain in her humble abode. The *shite* of *Umegae* is the spirit of a woman whose husband, a court musician, was killed by a rival. The *waki*, a traveling monk, prays for and consoles the grieving ghost. This is the role that Bashō envisioned for himself—a traveler who communes with the spirits of the dead.

The inscription on Hozumi's painting, with Bashō's haiku, left, and a passage from Umegae, *right.*

Pacifying the Dead

As mentioned earlier, many of noh's protagonists are the spirits of defeated warriors and other social outcasts. Even in the case of illustrious military leaders, the focus is on their tragic demise rather than their glorious victories. They are tortured souls in need of salvation. It is easy to see why Bashō, a native of the defeated and persecuted province of Iga, might sympathize with such characters.

It may be less clear at first why the Tokugawa shogunate, a military dictatorship, would share this interest in vanquished warriors. In fact, the shogunate embraced this genre of noh as a means of pacifying the restless spirits of slain enemy soldiers, lest they wreak havoc and destabilize the government. (As I explain below, the fear of vengeful spirits has been a powerful force in Japanese history and culture.)

This background offers an additional layer of insight into Bashō's best-known work, *Oku no hosomichi* (*The Narrow Road to the Deep North*), a prose and haiku account of a journey that Bashō undertook with his disciple, Kawai Sora, in 1689. Departing on foot from Edo in late March, Bashō reached the northeastern town of Hiraizumi (in present-day Iwate prefecture) and then journeyed back down along the Sea of Japan coast before ultimately arriving in Ōgaki (in present-day Gifu prefecture). Bashō worked on the text of *Oku* for five years, and it was only published posthumously, in 1702.

Oku reads very much like a travel diary, interspersed with poems inspired by the sights encountered along the way. But anyone who attempts to retrace Bashō's steps will realize that much of the account is fiction. In essence, *Oku* is a guidebook to the Deep North of Bashō's imagination. I have likened it to a role-playing video game in which Bashō embarks on an adventure-filled journey to meet dead poets and other figures from the past. The game has no fight scenes, but players can engage with historical personages, console grieving spirits, and enjoy the seasonal attractions of each famous place, with all its historical, religious, and literary associations. The object of the game is not to defeat an enemy or find a hidden treasure, as in an ordinary video game. It is to bring peace to troubled souls.

As I have argued, Bashō saw himself as an itinerant monk with a mission to lift such spirits from their misery and quell their rage. Moreover, I believe there was one particular soul he had in mind when he set out on his journey: Minamoto no Yoshitsune (1159–89), the tragic hero of the Genpei War, which ended the Heian period and ushered in an era of military rule under the Kamakura shogunate (1185–1333). I would even posit that the pacification of Yoshitsune's soul was a secret mission assigned to Bashō by the Tokugawa shogunate. After all, it can hardly be pure coincidence that the poet set out on his famed journey on the five hundredth anniversary of Yoshitsune's death, and that Bashō's primary destination was Hiraizumi, where the young general breathed his last.

The idea of appeasing angry souls might be dismissed as superstition today, but it still had great meaning in Bashō's day. Throughout

Japanese history, natural disasters, civil unrest, and other calamities had been attributed to vengeful spirits, or *onryō*, such as those of the ninth-century scholar-official Sugawara Michizane, who died in exile, and Taira no Masakado, killed after leading an unsuccessful revolt against the government in the tenth century. But perhaps the most malicious and violent of such spirits was that of Emperor Sutoku (r. 1123–42), who lost a struggle over the imperial succession and was banished to the remote province of Sanuki (now Kagawa prefecture), where he died in 1164.

Partly at the urging of the poet and monk Saigyō, the exiled emperor undertook to copy the five Mahayana Buddhist sutras, a task that took three years to complete. Sutoku sent the copied sutras to Kyoto, but the imperial court refused to accept them. According to legend, Sutoku became infuriated, bit off his own tongue, and bled to death, cursing the imperial family. Transforming himself into a demonic *tengu*, he proceeded to wreak vengeance down through the ages.

The efforts of successive emperors to pacify Sutoku's rage continued right up to modern times. Shiramine Shrine in Kyoto, dedicated to the kami of Emperor Sutoku, was planned by Emperor Kōmei (r. 1846–67) and completed by Emperor Meiji prior to his enthronement. In advance of the Tokyo Olympic Games of 1964, which coincided with the eight hundredth anniversary of Sutoku's death, Emperor Shōwa traveled to Sakaide in Kagawa prefecture, the site of Sutoku's mausoleum, to conduct Shintō rites and pray for the success of the games.

Just as the imperial family saw Emperor Sutoku's curse as a constant menace, the Tokugawa shogunate feared the wrath of the fallen hero Minamoto no Yoshitsune (1159–89). A military genius, Yoshitsune led the Minamoto forces to victory in the Genpei War, allowing his older half-brother, Minamoto no Yoritomo, to take power in 1185. But Yoritomo suspected Yoshitsune of plotting to usurp his power and issued an order for his capture. Yoshitsune fled to Hiraizumi, where he lived for a while under the protection of Fujiwara no Hidehira. Upon Hidehira's death, he was betrayed. Surrounded by the enemy, he took his own life.

The foundations of Tokugawa rule were already firmly established when Bashō set out on his journey to the North. The fifth shōgun, Tsunayoshi (r. 1680–1709), was free to pursue a variety of social, economic, administrative, and religious projects. Among these was the pacification of Yoshitsune's spirit.

In selecting someone to carry out this mission, Tsunayoshi's advisers (including the poet Kitamura Kigin) would doubtless have recalled the role played by Saigyō (1118–90), a famed poet and itinerant monk, in pacifying the angry spirit of Emperor Sutoku. They would have been looking for someone of comparable stature to pacify Yoshitsune. A natural choice was Bashō, likewise regarded as the greatest poet of his time.

Bashō and his disciple Sora, with the poet dressed as a monk.

A famous painting of Bashō and Sora by Morikawa Kyoriku, Bashō's disciple, shows the poet dressed as a monk, holding a bamboo hat in front of him. A bamboo hat held waist high is a standard feature of Saigyō iconography. (Of course, this is also the typical garb of the *waki* in a noh play.) I believe this painting portrayed Bashō in the role to which he aspired.

Off to the "Deep North"

Of course, Bashō also had his own reasons for embarking on the journey.

At the peak of his professional career, when he was earning a comfortable living as a poetry teacher, Bashō had moved from Nihonbashi in the bustling heart of Edo to a tiny hut in the relatively undeveloped Fukagawa district. The move had cost him many of his wealthy patrons, but it signaled his resolve to focus on his art and earn the approval of the great poets of yore, disdaining worldly goods and honors. It was an impulse consistent with the ethos of renunciation so often expressed by the *waki* near the start of a noh play.

After setting off from Fukagawa, Bashō walked some 140 kilometers in just four days—an average of over 30 kilometers a day—to reach his first destination, Nikkō (in present-day Tochigi prefecture). Nikkō is a doubly sacred site, known not only for an important Buddhist temple to Kannon (the bodhisattva of mercy) but also for Tōshōgū Shrine, dedicated to the first shōgun Tokugawa Ieyasu, as well as Ieyasu's mausoleum.

From Nikkō, Bashō headed north to Nasu on what may be the most mysterious leg of the entire 2,400-kilometer journey. Nasu was the site of an old willow described in one of Saigyō's poems. It is also the setting of two noh plays, *Sesshōseki* and *Yugyō yanagi*, based on Saigyō's poem. It was thus a must-see destination for Bashō. To reach the fabled willow, we learn, he takes a broad, straight path. This is odd, since the *waki* in *Yugyō yanagi* is explicitly told by the old man (*shite*) to take the narrow path if he wishes to find Saigyō's willow.

Then, lo and behold, Bashō is stopped in his tracks by a rainstorm. The afternoon sky grows dark, as if night had fallen. With this technique—common in noh—Bashō pulls readers into an alternate universe. He spends the night in a farmhouse, and when he awakens in the morning, the wide, straight road has disappeared, replaced by a web of narrow, tangled paths. Welcome to the world of *mugen* noh!

At a loss as to how to proceed, Bashō asks directions of a local farmer selling pinks and other flowers. Taking pity on Bashō, the man lends him his horse, saying, "Keep riding as far as he will go, and then just send him back." Two small children follow after Bashō. The little girl tells them her name is Kasane (which can mean "double"), an unusual and charming name. Inspired, Sora composes a poem: "Kasane to wa / yae nadeshiko no / na narubeshi" (Kasane must be the name / given the wild pink / with double petals). There are those who claim the haiku was actually written by Bashō, but what is clear in either case is that there is something extraordinary—almost otherworldly—about the girl. One can imagine a noh play based on this interlude featuring a *shite* who turns out to be the spirit of the flower.

Threads in the Tapestry

Utai, as I have mentioned, was widely practiced and enjoyed by commoners as well as samurai in the Edo period. It was a vast repository of shared knowledge from which people could draw to express deep and complex sentiments. For haikai poets, *utai* merited comparison with the *Tale of Genji* as a source of inspiration and literary allusions. Noh itself draws heavily on *Genji*, and *Genji* is full of references and allusions to earlier literature, especially the poetry collected in such imperial anthologies as the mid-eighth-century *Man'yōshū* and the early tenth-century *Kokin wakashū*. Japanese literature is built from such layered, interwoven threads of literary allusion, and *Oku no hosomichi* is part of that tapestry.

It stands to reason, therefore, that a knowledge of *utai* can enhance one's understanding and appreciation of Bashō's verses. A notable example is the poem he wrote while resting in the shade of Saigyō's willow tree: "Ta ichimai / uete tachisaru / yanagi kana" (Only when a whole field of rice / had been sown did I leave / [Saigyō's] willow tree). Because the poem is without a subject in the Japanese, there has been some debate as to exactly who it was that left the willow tree. But when the poem is envisioned as a scene in a *mugen* noh play, the answer becomes obvious. It is Bashō himself, playing the role of *waki*. We see him resting beneath the willow, singing lines from the play *Yugyō yanagi* and watching young women planting seedlings. He grows drowsy, and the spirit of the willow appears in *shite*'s garb, dancing slowly before him. It vanishes, and he awakens from his dream to find that a whole field of rice has been planted while he napped.

The word *waki* derives from *wakeru* (to divide). The *waki* straddles two different realms, the physical universe in which we live and the world beyond, and is therefore able to hear the voices of troubled spirits and offer them release through prayer. With the words "Tabibito to waga na yobaren" (Let my name be traveler), Bashō was announcing his intent to journey between this world and the next, much like a *waki*, communing with the illustrious spirits of the past and finding his place within Japan's long, unbroken spiritual and artistic lineage.

Masaoka Shiki and Takahama Kyoshi—both members of Sōseki's circle—were among Meiji Japan's leading champions of the haiku form. Both, as we have seen, were devotees of noh.

Kyoshi viewed haiku as the epitome of "heavenly" literature, a kind of poetic expression that transports us to a realm of beauty where the pain and misery of our worldly existence are forgotten, however briefly. He placed noh dancing on a similar plane.

Virtually every noh play climaxes with a dance by the *shite*. The dance embodies the spirit's release as it transcends the torment of its human existence. Noh actors who have portrayed such beings countless times in their careers cannot but see life and death, as Bashō and Shiki did, as part of a larger continuum.

Chapter VII

Engaging the Imagination

Participatory Theater

The noh stage has no proscenium arch or drop curtain separating the actors from the audience. This is consistent with the active and integral role audiences are expected to play as theatrical co-creators. Noh, perhaps more than any other performing art, relies on the audience's imagination to bring literary works to life in three dimensions—a demand that can deliver an incomparably rich and rewarding experience for both performer and viewer.

A number of popular Japanese theatrical genres have continued this tradition of recreating a literary world in three dimensions. Today's so-called 2.5-dimensional musicals—stage adaptations of popular anime, manga, or video games—are a prime example. Among the pioneering productions in this genre were *Tenisu no ōji-sama* (*The Prince of Tennis*) and *Yowamushi pedaru* (Weakling Pedal), which have become great hits with the fans of the original manga series. A more immediate ancestor of this genre is the Takarazuka all-female revue, founded over a century ago, whose lavish Broadway-style musical productions are often adapted from *shōjo* manga targeting the young female demographic. Takarazuka fans are particularly renowned for their devotion to individual stars of the stage, the embodiments of a cherished fantasy world.

Fans back in Zeami's day were just as obsessed with their favorite *sarugaku* (noh) stars. Zeami recounts an incident in which so many onlookers squeezed into a gallery to watch an acrobatic boy actor of eight or nine that the multistory seating structure collapsed. During a performance at Kyoto's Kitano Shrine, zealous fans climbed the roofs of nearby buildings to get a glimpse of Inuō, an older rival to Zeami. As the fan base grew, so did the fanaticism, turning *sarugaku* actors into larger-than-life heroes, the equivalent of today's rock and movie stars.

Virtual Voyages

Unlike today's popular theatrical genres, however, noh does not bombard audiences with visual information. People expecting to see elaborate stage sets or outlandish costumes are likely to be disappointed. But those ready to engage their creativity and suspend disbelief are sure to be richly rewarded. With a bare stage and just a handful of actors, noh can tap into one's imagination and transport one to a distant land. (This was no doubt an attractive proposition in premodern times, when most people lived their entire lives close to home.)

A good example is the play *Unrin-in*, adapted from *Ise monogatari* (*Tales of Ise*)—a Heian-period collection of poems and narratives about courtly romance and adventure that takes readers on a journey from Kyoto in western Honshū to Miyagi in the northeast by way of Shinano (present-day Nagano prefecture), Suruga (central Shizuoka prefecture), and Musashino (around modern-day Tokyo). The play itself is set in the grounds of a Kyoto temple named Unrin-in, where an avid reader of the *Tales of Ise* meets the spirit of its protagonist and purported author, the ninth-century courtier-poet Ariwara no Narihira, and is made privy to the work's secrets.

According to *Kokin denju*, an ancient commentary on Heian-period poetry originally transmitted orally, the various locations described in the *Tales of Ise* were replicated in miniature within the imperial palace gardens. Unlike the expansive, geometric, and symmetrical gardens of the West, Japanese gardens are built on undulating terrain and are meant to be viewed from a meandering path that presents one carefully composed scene after another. Members of the court could retrace Narihira's steps without leaving the palace grounds.

A surviving example of this type of garden design is Rikugien in Tokyo, built by Yanagisawa Yoshiyasu (1658–1714), a high-ranking shogunal official. This renowned landscape garden presents condensed views of scenic spots featured in poems from the *Man'yōshū* and the *Kokin wakashū*, each paired with a stone pillar engraved with an excerpt from the poem. For Yanagisawa, a man of culture with a deep knowledge of poetry, Rikugien must have been like a private theme park that allowed him to visit the scenes of his favorite poems anytime. Armed with some of that background knowledge, present-day visitors to the garden can likewise enjoy a virtual journey to those destinations, all without the aid of digital technology. It is a kind of augmented reality generated from within.

In a similar way, knowledgeable noh audiences are quickly transported to distant places via the "augmented reality" of their own imagination. Some devotees can embark on a virtual voyage simply by singing a few lines of their favorite *utai*.

This does not mean that noh is incompatible with the use of digital technology to enhance the viewing experience. Noh professionals are frequently approached by researchers exploring the application of noh to virtual reality and vice versa. One group has begun studying ways in which viewers' experience of noh could be augmented through the use of smart glasses. The idea is not to add visual information, such as a 3D or 360-degree scenic backdrop, but rather to stimulate the brain's natural ability to generate augmented reality.

Stripping Away the Detail

The bareness of the noh stage is perhaps the most eloquent statement of the importance noh places on the imagination. Unlike kabuki, noh does not use stage sets or theatrical scenery to depict the play's setting; for 650 years, the only thing adorning a noh stage has been the painting of a pine tree on the rear wall. The Tokugawa shogunate could easily have used its financial resources to create more elaborate sets for noh, but it did not.

Why this Spartan simplicity? In fact, it is the bareness of the stage that allows the imagination to travel to another place and time. Like the austerity of a Zen garden, it induces an interactive response through the very absence of detail. So it is that the audience "sees" the full moon or "hears" the crashing of waves. The minimalist stage is central to noh's success, which is doubtless the reason its structure was left intact even after it moved indoors following the Meiji Restoration.

The other key element noh relies on to animate the imagination is *utai*. Like the poems inscribed in stone at Rikugien garden, the lines of a play can instantly transport a knowledgeable audience to distant places and periods in time. This sort of conjuration is not unique to noh; the power of the spoken or sung word to summon up a fictional world and bring an audience to tears or keep them on the edge of their seats is also at the core of such quintessentially Japanese art forms as bunraku, *rakugo, rōkyoku, heikyoku, gidayū,* and *kōdan.*

Still, *utai* may have the edge in that it draws so heavily on Japan's rich tradition of classical poetry, or *waka.* The places referred to in *utai* are inextricably associated with *waka* that, in turn, refer to older verses about the same location, so that the mere mention of a place name can elicit layers and layers of imagery and emotion.

The power of *waka* to stir the imagination is augmented by the fact that in the past these poems were sung or chanted—as is still the custom at the New Year's poetry readings held at the Imperial Palace. This was most likely true of haiku as well, as suggested by Bashō's inscription of his own poem alongside a passage from the noh play *Umegae* on the painting discussed in chapter 6.[1] The lines from *Umegae* are accompanied by notations showing how they should be sung; one can assume, then, that the haiku was also meant to be vocalized.

A Lifelong Friend

It seems to me that modern media have undermined people's ability to fill in the blanks with their own imagination. With instant

---

1. See page 69.

entertainment just a phone tap away, it is small wonder that people's attention spans and imaginative powers appear to be declining.

Fortunately, words still have the power to trigger vivid mental images and associations. The fact that I could "see" the moon at the very first noh performance I attended, when I had no intellectual understanding of noh, demonstrates its power to stimulate the imagination. Perhaps the first requirement for a noh fan is simply to allow one's imagination to follow wherever the performance leads—to be mesmerized by the actor's gliding movements, stirred by the ferocity or beauty of a mask, or roused by the intensity of the music.

Audiences unaccustomed to using their imagination may find their first noh performance utterly boring. It is not an uncommon reaction. Noh will not appeal to people who merely sit back and expect to be entertained; it requires viewers to engage actively and meet it halfway. At that midway point is where the imagination kicks in, revealing that which the eye cannot see. The reward can be a magical and moving experience that enhances our connection with the past and deepens our understanding and appreciation of the human experience.

Noh is not a commodity to be consumed and discarded or measured by box office receipts. It is more like a companion with whom one willingly shares one's life. To better appreciate its nuanced expression, I recommend taking singing (*utai*) or dancing (*shimai*) lessons. If a qualified teacher is unavailable, you can start by just reading a text aloud. Visiting the place described in a play can also stir the imagination and help bring the story to life. Such steps, I am confident, will go a long way toward turning noh into a close and lifelong friend.

CHAPTER VIII

WHY STUDY NOH?

In the first chapter of this book, I discussed some of the ways in which the appreciation and study of noh can benefit contemporary society. In this final chapter, I would like to focus on the way noh singing and dance can enrich our lives on a personal level. I begin with some of my own observations regarding the health benefits of noh and proceed to an overview of the "fifteen virtues of *utai*" lauded since premodern times before concluding with some advice to those thinking of embarking on their own noh journey.

Physical Health and Fitness

I once had an opportunity to teach *utai* and *suriashi*—a technique of moving across the floor without lifting one's feet—to schoolchildren at a neighborhood temple. A few months later, a number of them reported that they had been chosen for the school's relay team. This was remarkable, as they were all relatively small for their age and not known for their speed. Now they were able to run faster. According to their parents, they were also eating more and taking fewer days off school. This got me thinking about noh's positive effects on health and fitness.

One thing I learned is that *suriashi* activates the psoas major and other core muscles. An examination of *shite* actor Tsumura Reijirō and myself, carried out on a Japanese television program, showed that both of us had the psoas major of someone much younger. Tsumura, a septuagenarian, had the muscles of a thirty-year-old; mine (I was fifty at the time) were like those of a man in his twenties.

Over the past decade or so, I have been leading a group of *hiki-komori*—people who have withdrawn from social life—on walking tours of the route the poet Matsuo Bashō took on his journey to the Deep North. For a few months before we depart, I teach *suriashi* to these recluses. Some of them have been cooped up at home for twenty years or more, but after they learn *suriashi*, they are able to walk eight hours a day on trips lasting five to ten days. As a *waki* actor, I do not teach dance (which is performed by the *shite*), but I feel confident that practicing *shimai* would confer additional health and fitness benefits.

Mental Focus and Equanimity

The practice of noh can also enhance mental focus. Whenever I find myself distracted or unable to concentrate, I put down what I am doing and sing *utai* for about fifteen minutes. When I go back to work, I find that my mind is clearer, and I am better able to focus. Deep, controlled breathing is doubtless one aspect of this effect.

Breath control forms the core of many meditation techniques. But beginners often find it hard to clear their minds of distracting thoughts just by concentrating on the breath. The harder they try, the busier their minds become. This is because they have nothing concrete on which to concentrate. In Zen, novices try to get around the problem by counting their breaths. *Utai* focuses the mind on text, rhythm, and melody, while at the same time conferring the benefits of deep breathing.

Vigorous vocalization forces us to take deeper breaths and strengthens the diaphragm, enhancing our overall health and sense of well-being. (Conversely, when we are feeling unwell, our respiration tends to become shallow.) Vocalization is also a primal and time-honored means of relieving stress.

Oda Nobunaga famously sang and danced a short piece in a genre closely related to noh before the decisive Battle of Okehazama in 1560 (see chapter 1). Greatly outnumbered in troop strength, he must have been under enormous pressure, knowing that defeat would mean not only his own death but also the annihilation of his family and the demise of his clan. The dance and the accompanying song, which requires deep, powerful breaths, helped to calm his nerves and transmute his anxiety into explosive energy. In fact, that sublimated stress was doubtless the fuel that powered Nobunaga's superhuman feats on the battlefield.

Similar anecdotes abound. One concerns my teacher's father, who committed ritual suicide the day after Japan's surrender in World War II. In addition to being head of the Shundō school of *waki* actors, he was a Shintō priest who had performed ceremonies for countless young men going off to battle. On the day before he took his own life, he visited a family to whom he was deeply indebted. At the train station on the way home, he began singing and dancing a piece called *Shōjō* with great intensity, as if to atone for his role in the needless deaths of so many young soldiers.

The forty-seven loyal rōnin who avenged the death of their master in the eighteenth-century Akō Incident are said to have sung a section of the play *Rashōmon* on the eve of their attack against their nemesis. The poet Takahama Kyoshi sang for his mentor Masaoka Shiki as the latter lay dying of tuberculosis. The combination of concentration and deep breathing demanded by *utai* has a bracing and calming effect that can help one rise to the most demanding occasions with strength and equanimity. This is doubtless one reason noh was embraced by the samurai class in premodern Japan and by so many of Japan's political and economic leaders after the Meiji Restoration.

Nonverbal Communication

Another way in which noh answered the needs of the samurai was by helping them cultivate the ability to communicate nonverbally. Warriors must anticipate their comrades' movements on the battlefield if they are to function as an effective fighting force. (The same is true of participants in team sports.) Of course, commands can be conveyed with audible and visual signals. Ideally, though, soldiers should know what is expected of them without being told, moving organically like the cells of a single organism.

Noh is performed without the benefit of a conductor or director. Moreover, unlike opera or Western theater, it largely dispenses with ensemble rehearsals—and this despite the fact that the *shite*, *waki*, and musicians are all trained in different schools. A single *mōshiawase*—a rehearsal of the sections involving the *shite*—is normally held a day or two before the performance, but even this is sometimes skipped.

How, then, do the performers coordinate with one another? For one thing, they have trained and practiced so diligently on their own that they are capable of adapting their performances as the circumstances demand. But another important factor is the role of *komi*. Narrowly defined, *komi* refers to the silent beats between the drum strikes and the *kakegoe* (vocalized cues) of the percussionists, which are counted in the mind (or, as the Japanese say, in the *hara*, or belly). *Komi* in the broadest sense is an internalized conception of the play as performed on stage, including its pacing and emphasis. By discussing their internalized notions of the play prior to the performance, performers can dispense with rehearsals.

If there are enough connoisseurs in the audience, the *komi* can pervade the entire theater, giving the impression that the performer and viewer have coalesced and are moving and breathing as one. Such a sense of unity is also the ideal for military commanders and troops on the battlefield. This is surely another reason that training in *utai*, *shimai*, *komi*, and other aspects of noh was made mandatory for members of the ruling warrior class.

Balancing Yin and Yang

Noh dances are composed of a series of formal *kata*, conventionalized moves with no specific meaning. Other Japanese dance forms, such as *Nihon buyō*, are composed of gestures (*furi*) that mimic the motions of daily life or natural phenomena. Many non-Japanese dance forms also incorporate movements with specific meanings; hula, for example, dramatizes the words of songs with gestures signifying phenomena like rainfall or emotions like sadness. The *kata* from which noh dancing is built, by contrast, have no inherent representational or expressive meaning.

The climax of many noh plays is the *mai* (dance) performed in the second act to instrumental accompaniment, without the chorus. The individual *kata* that make up these dances are essentially the same from play to play. Viewers accustomed to Western dramaturgy may look for meaning in each step or gesture and, failing to find it, may lose interest in the dance. But once they let go of the notion that each movement must mean something, they will find themselves mesmerized by the refinement and beauty of the dancer's movements and the flow of energy expanding and contracting onstage.

Noh dances are generally built from pairs of *kata* that embody the principles of yin and yang. The most common sequence consists of the two *kata* known as *shikake* (or *sashikomi* in the Kanze school) and *hiraki*. *Shikake*, which embodies yang, is performed by taking a few steps forward while raising one's right arm forward. *Hiraki*, embodying yin, involves taking a few steps back while bringing both arms to one's side. The pairing of *kata* in this manner allows practitioners to balance their energy levels without a conscious effort. The balancing of positive and negative energy is a key concept in traditional East Asian thought and Eastern medicine. In premodern times, the practice of noh was one means by which members of the warrior class, which collectively governed the nation, maintained an internal and external balance between yin and yang.

Strengthening the Voice

An obvious benefit of studying *utai* is that it will improve your voice. Back in the days when noh was normally performed outdoors, actors needed to develop a loud, booming voice just to be heard. A resonant voice is still important, as microphones are never used in noh, not even by the oldest performers.

I suffered from asthma as a child, and when I first began studying *utai* with Kaburaki Mineo, my voice was still very weak. Surely no one then could have imagined that I would someday become a professional noh actor. At every lesson, my teacher would exhort me, "Louder! Sing from your *hara*!" But I had no idea how to do that, and needless to say, he never explained the technique.

I persevered, however, and one day I noticed that my voice had become much more powerful. Initially, I had been singing just from my throat, which had made me hoarse. Forced to improvise, I learned not to rely on my throat but to use my entire body to vocalize.

Many of my own students today are people who regularly speak in front of audiences. They report that their voices carry much better than before and that they can talk far longer without getting hoarse. Studying *utai* teaches one how to use one's whole body to support the voice. The result is not just greater volume but also a richer, more resonant voice.

The Fifteen Virtues

Since premodern times, devotees of noh have extolled its benefits, with a focus on how it can enrich its practitioners intellectually, emotionally, and spiritually. The practice of *utai* was seen as a convenient means by which the samurai could cultivate Confucian virtues, erudition, and other sought-after qualities. These wide-ranging benefits are summed up in the "fifteen virtues of *utai*" attributed to Hosokawa Fujitaka (1534–1610), founder of the clan that would later rule the Kumamoto domain.[1]

1. Acquaint yourself with famous spots without going there

In chapter 7, I described how noh plays like *Unrin-in* transport viewers to remote locales rich in sentimental and literary significance. The singing of *utai*, similarly, allows one to travel in spirit to Japan's most famous and picturesque destinations without leaving the comfort of one's home.

---

1. Some versions of the list cite only ten virtues, while others boast as many as thirty.

2. Strike up friendships while far from home

A perfect example of this second "virtue" is the episode I introduced in chapter 3 about two perfect strangers singing *Hagoromo* on the streets of Kanazawa and instantly developing a deep rapport. In this way and others, *utai* makes an excellent travel companion. Most noh schools publish miniature editions of individual plays that can be carried in one's pocket.

3. Learn poetry without rigorous study

Waka, the chief poetic form of ancient Japan, is one of this country's great artistic achievements, capturing the beauty and poignancy of life in all its transience. The *Kokin wakashū*, a tenth-century imperial anthology of Japanese poetry, credits *waka* with the power to move heaven and earth, stir the emotions of spirits and kami, unite the hearts of men and women, and calm the passions of fierce warriors. *Utai* is a treasure trove of famous *waka*, and the study of *utai* is a pleasurable shortcut to familiarity with these classics.

4. Appreciate nature without versifying

Since ancient times, poetry has served to awaken a deeper appreciation of nature and our place within it. The ability to compose verse while contemplating the full moon or falling blossoms was once viewed as a key measure of an individual's depth and refinement. The singing of *utai* functions in much the same way, imbuing these sights with poignant meaning and prompting us to reflect more deeply on the nature of things.

5. Find peace in quiet seclusion

The insatiable desire to be liked and validated by others has fueled widespread addiction to social media in recent years, with the result that many now complain of social-media fatigue. We socialize with people we do not particularly like just to please them or to avoid being alone, which ends up exacerbating our loneliness. Perhaps what we really need is the courage to be by ourselves. The empty hours of a rainy spring day or a long autumn night fly by swiftly when one is lost in the pleasures of *utai*.

6. Dispel melancholy without medication

Belting out an *utai* piece is an excellent means of alleviating stress, as I mentioned above, and it is also a good way of beating the blues. Unlike pharmaceuticals, moreover, *utai* has no side effects. Singing *utai* in an upright seated posture has much the same effect as seated meditation, and it is arguably more effective in releasing pent-up anger and frustration.

7. Earn an unexpected seat of honor

In Japan, anyone with the ability to grace an auspicious occasion with the appropriate *utai* is likely to be treated as a valued guest—particularly nowadays, when such people are in short supply. Even in other countries, a noh practitioner is apt to enjoy special marks of hospitality, including a seat among the honored guests (a benefit closely related to the next "virtue").

8. Rub shoulders with people in high places

Becoming a noh actor has given me the opportunity to meet and converse intimately with a great many prominent people, including presidents of foreign countries and many of the scholars, writers, and movie directors whom I had long admired.

9. Learn the lessons of the ancients before you are ancient

Utai draws liberally on allegories and other instructive content from the Chinese and Japanese classics, giving one ready access to their timeless wisdom. Singing *utai* is a good way to absorb and contemplate these lessons so that one can apply them as the situation demands.

10. *Admire great beauties from a safe distance*

Romantic love is a great source of joy and vitality, but it can also be messy and hurtful. Perhaps this is why so many young people today shun such relationships, preferring to surround themselves with their favorite manga or anime characters. For *otaku* and other introverts, I recommend *utai*, which offers the thrill of knowing such legendary beauties as the poetess Ono no Komachi and the Tang-dynasty imperial consort Yang Guifei—not to mention the fetching heroes and heroines of *Genji monogatari* (*Tale of Genji*)—with none of the complications.

11. *Learn martial skills without training*

A martial-arts expert I once spoke to expressed his admiration for the way noh actors carry themselves, quipping that he would not care to tangle with one. While I doubt that any noh actor would relish such a confrontation either, his comments underscored the physical and mental qualities acquired through noh training and how much they have in common with the skills developed in the martial arts.

12. *Experience war without fighting*

Warfare features prominently in many of the world's great myth cycles and epics, and Japan's oldest surviving literary work, the *Kojiki* (*Record of Ancient Matters*), is no exception. Tales of martial feats and heroism in the face of death are gripping and inspiring. When such scenes are sung as *utai*, one can almost hear the shouts of soldiers, the drumming of hoofbeats, and the whizzing of arrows. Such pieces also bring home the horror and tragedy of war, reflecting the undercurrent of anti-war sentiment in much of the noh repertoire.

13. Receive divine blessings without praying

Those who think of prayer as the heartfelt invocation of a higher being may take issue with this, but my own sense is that most people who pray at Buddhist temples and Shintō shrines nowadays are just requesting handouts. If there is any truth to the saying "blessed are the pure in heart," then singing *utai* with sincerity should have greater efficacy than a hundred such half-hearted prayers.

14. Learn the teachings of Buddhism without reading the scriptures

Buddhism plays an ever-diminishing role in the lives of the Japanese people. For the vast majority, temples are places to visit on sightseeing trips or when attending funerals; the deeper teachings of Buddhism seem remote and inaccessible. In *utai*, Buddhist doctrine is conveyed in vivid, meaningful terms through the medium of noh's memorable characters.

15. Cut a fine figure without taking great pains

Training in *utai* and *shimai* can help people look and feel better naturally by enhancing their health, fitness, posture, and poise.

Getting Started

As we have seen, noh has a great deal to offer people of all ages. Yet the fact is that the "uninitiated" tend to find it remote and unapproachable. They say they have no idea what to see first, where to buy tickets, or what to wear to a performance—let alone how to embark on formal study.

In a sense, this feeling of exclusivity is only natural, given noh's former status as a pastime reserved for society's elite. And perhaps it is not entirely a bad thing. Noh is a unique and precious artistic tradition, nurtured over 650 years, not a disposable commodity for mass consumption. The goal should be not to popularize it but to make it available to those who seek the sort of enrichment it offers.

The samurai saw such value in noh that they sought to keep it for themselves. Those same qualities are what make noh such a precious cultural resource today. But its riches lie beneath the surface and are truly revealed only to those willing to dig down a bit. Those are the people I hope to reach with this book.

I am an actor, not a scholar. I have introduced Zeami's ideas and the historical development of noh from my particular vantage point as a *waki* actor, and my interpretation reflects my personal experience as well as my extensive readings on the subject. I would encourage readers to form their own ideas by studying noh themselves.

For those who simply wish to learn more about noh, there are plenty of readily accessible resources in print and online. One might even start with some of the novels and manga mentioned in chapter 3. The appendix provides a more comprehensive listing.

That said, the best way to penetrate to the essence of noh is to take the leap and begin training under a qualified instructor. It is only through physical immersion in this art form that one gains full access to its value, including the benefits I have described in this chapter. The appendix includes a list of resources for those seeking direct instruction.

How, one might ask, should one go about choosing the right teacher? When Natsume Sōseki was asked why he chose to study with Shimogakari Hōshō, he made it clear that he had put little thought into the matter. "No one who has not already studied noh has the discernment to choose among schools and so forth," he pointed out. "These things are generally determined by your circumstances and the people around you." That said, it worked out quite well for Sōseki in the end.

Similarly, it was luck, more than choice, that led me to my own teacher Kaburaki Mineo (who passed away in June 2017). Had I attended more noh performances before I began studying, I might have knocked on someone else's door. Kaburaki sensei did not perform as frequently as some *waki* actors, since he was also a Shintō priest. By the same token, however, he was able to teach me about Shintō and Japanese mythology as well as noh. He also had more time to devote to my training.

Once you start taking lessons with someone, I would strongly urge you to stay the course. It can take decades of study to discriminate among various schools and teachers. Flitting from one instructor to another is not the answer. Etymologically, the Japanese word for "lesson," *keiko*, connotes deep reverence for the past. Recognize your teacher as the successor to a long tradition of excellence extending back to Kan'ami and Zeami and follow him in that spirit.

Your textbooks for the study of *utai* will be softcover *utaibon* bound in the traditional style. They contain the text of each play, along with notations indicating how passages should be sung. They invariably have large margins, providing plenty of room to scribble your teacher's instructions and any personal memos. As you continue your lessons, your personal collection of *utaibon* will grow, as will your knowledge and memories of the pieces you learned over the years.

My hope is that many more people will come to recognize noh's myriad benefits and join me in spreading the word about this priceless treasure.

Appendix

The following is a beginner's guide for people interested in delving deeper into noh. It starts with some pointers for those wishing to attend noh performances, proceeds to tips for prospective students, provides key information resources, and concludes with an overview of some regional sites of historic, cultural, and aesthetic interest.

Attending Noh

Finding an opportunity to watch noh live should be your top priority. During your first few outings, you may find the story hard to follow and even doze off during the performance. Don't be discouraged. For some, noh is an acquired taste. But the more you watch and learn, the more you will find to love.

Buying Tickets

Tickets are sold at the theaters where the performances are held and through ticket agencies. The actors on the program are another major source for tickets. An English-language schedule of noh performances around Japan can be found online at the the-NOH.com website (https://www.the-noh.com/en/schedule/index.html). The websites of the individual noh schools and theaters usually publish their own calendars of performances covering the next few months. In addition, with more and more noh actors writing blogs and using social media, a simple web search will generally turn up a wealth of information.

For those who read Japanese, the monthly *Nohgaku Times* (covering all schools) and the newsletters published by individual schools are good print sources of performance and ticket information.

The seats facing the front of the stage, called *shōmen*, are typically the most expensive. Those to the left side (stage right) are called *waki-shōmen*, and the wedge-shaped area in between these two sections is called *naka-shōmen*. Seasoned noh-goers will have their personal seating preferences, but first-time viewers would probably do well to choose a *shōmen* seat.

What to See First

When targeting non-Japanese audiences or novices, organizers often select plays that are flashy or visually appealing—*Tsuchigumo*, *Momiji-gari*, or *Funabenkei*, for example. But some first-time viewers are more deeply stirred by slower-moving masterpieces, such as *Matsukaze* and *Izutsu*. These *katsura mono* (discussed on page 36) may be for you if you are eager to jump right in and savor the profound, mysterious beauty unique to noh.

Fans of classical Japanese literature might like to start with one of the ten plays based on *Genji monogatari* (*Tale of Genji*), such as *Aoi no ue*, *Hajitomi*, or *Yūgao*. *Ise monogatari* (*Tales of Ise*) is the basis for *Unrin-in*, *Kakitsubata*, and *Izutsu*, while *Heike monogatari* (*Tale of the Heike*) supplied the inspiration for *Yorimasa*, *Atsumori*, *Ataka*, and many other noh plays. All of these works are performed quite regularly, attesting to their popularity.

Those with short attention spans might do well to avoid some of the longer plays, such as *Yugyō yanagi* (even though it was one of Bashō's favorites). The longest play in the repertoire may be *Obasute*, which can last for over two and a half hours.

Studying Up

You can derive considerable enjoyment from a noh performance even without any background knowledge; indeed, first-time viewers are often discouraged from trying to "make sense" of everything. That said, the archaic, literary language of noh is difficult to follow even for native Japanese speakers, and program notes do not always include summaries of the plays being performed. To ensure that your first encounter with noh is not your last, it is probably best to go equipped with at least a basic grasp of the plot. This should not be difficult, as the stories are generally very simple. If you have access to the text of the play, reading through it beforehand will allow you to follow the action and will greatly enhance your viewing experience. Each year in Tokyo, I organize a program consisting of a noh performance preceded by around five workshops, in which I provide the participants with all the knowledge they need to fully enjoy their outing. Details can be found on my website, Wa to Wa (http://watowa.net).

What to Wear

You may dress as formally or casually as you like for a noh performance, but dressing up a bit might put you in a more receptive frame of mind. For some fans, attending noh is a much-anticipated opportunity to wear their kimono. (Those with a particularly large wardrobe will choose colors and designs suggestive of the plays on the program.) Whatever you wear, you may want to consider that the thermostat for the seating area is set slightly higher than in most public venues, since noh audiences tend to be older on the whole.

At many theaters, performances start a little before noon and end in the late afternoon. Some theaters have a cafeteria, but many viewers prefer to bring a sandwich or other refreshments that they can eat in the lobby during intermission.

Houselights are kept on during noh performances. Brighter lighting means that you can read the *utai* text (usually sold in the lobby) as you watch the play.

Spotlight on the Dance

The *mai* (dance), performed in the second act to instrumental accompaniment, is the climax of most noh plays. Sometimes, its impact is such that the rest of play seems ancillary. Even if you sleep through everything else, you will not want to miss the *mai*. As I explained in chapter 8, avoid searching for meaning in each step or gesture. It is enough to appreciate the beauty, grace, and energy of the dancer's movements.

Studying Noh

If after a few performances you are eager to dive deeper, then it is time to think about taking lessons. The following is a simple guide to locating a teacher and embarking on the next phase of your noh journey.

What to Study

Many people start with *utai* (noh singing), which I discuss throughout this book. In that case, you will learn to sing entire pieces, including the dialogue. Others prefer to begin with *shimai*, which are short dance excerpts, each lasting several minutes, performed to the accompaniment of the *jiutai* (chorus). The next step after *shimai* is *maibayashi*, which is accompanied also by musical instruments. After a number of years studying *utai* and *shimai*, some go on to perform in a full-length noh play.

You might also choose to study any of the four *hayashi* instruments: *nōkan* (flute), *kotsuzumi* (shoulder drum), *ōtsuzumi* (hip drum), and *taiko* (stick drum). Some may be drawn to *kyōgen*, a form of comic drama that is performed alongside noh. While professional *shite* actors normally teach both *utai* and *shimai*, *waki* actors usually teach only *utai*.

Where to Study

The easiest way to find a teacher is to be introduced to one by a friend. Failing that, group classes are available at many community centers. If, after trying group lessons, you are interested in taking it to the next level, you can then opt for private classes. Inquiries about lessons may be made via the websites of the individual schools (see below), including mine, Shimogakari Hōshō (http://shimohou.com). (Unfortunately, I personally am unable to take on any more students at this time.) Hinoki Shoten, the publisher of texts for the Kanze and Kongō schools, and Wan'ya Shoten, which issues books for the Hōshō and Konparu schools, can also refer you to a teacher. The National Noh Theatre (see below) runs a professional training program for aspiring noh actors.

Websites of Major Schools/Branches and Publishers

Kanze school	https://kanze.net
Tessen-kai	http://www.tessen.org
Kyūkō-kai	https://yarai-nohgakudo.com
Umewaka Kennō-kai	http://www.umewakakennohkai.com
Umewaka-kai	https://umewaka.org
Hōshō school	http://www.hosho.or.jp
Konparu school	https://www.komparu-enmaikai.com
Kita school	http://kita-noh.com
Kongō school	http://www.kongou-net.com
Hinoki Shoten	https://www.hinoki-shoten.co.jp
Wan'ya Shoten	http://www.wanya.biz
Nōgaku Shorin	http://nohgakushorin.co.jp

How Much Does It Cost?

Lessons do not require a hefty initial investment. All you need to purchase up front will be the *utai* texts of the plays you are learning and a fan, both of which you can buy through your teacher. If you are going to learn *shimai*, you will need to purchase a pair of white *tabi* socks.

As for the lessons themselves, tuition will depend very much on the teacher and type of class you choose. Sometimes an enrollment fee is required. Many students also send semiannual courtesy gifts—often monetary—as a matter of custom. Other expenditures include recital fees, which vary according to the piece and role performed. Although participation in a recital is not mandatory, it is strongly encouraged; performing in front of an audience is the fastest path to improvement, a way of "cracking the shell" in the spirit of *shoshin* and breaking through to the next level.

Some may worry about having to buy a kimono and other pricey garments in order to take part in a recital. There is no need to splurge while you are still a novice. Older students are usually more than happy to lend their kimono. Contrary to popular belief, lessons in the traditional arts need not be prohibitively expensive.

Key Resources

The following is a list of resources to which fans and students can turn for more detailed information.

The-NOH.com
https://www.the-noh.com

This bilingual website is probably the world's most comprehensive online resource for noh, with a wealth of information available in English as well as Japanese. It contains detailed synopses and texts of major plays, a glossary of noh terms, and interesting anecdotes by professional actors. (I have contributed a number articles to the site myself.)

Kanazawa Noh Museum
https://www.kanazawa-noh-museum.gr.jp/english

This is the only museum in Japan dedicated exclusively to noh. Kanazawa was the seat of the Kaga domain, where the Hōshō school of noh flourished under the enthusiastic patronage of the Maeda clan during the Edo period. Following the Meiji Restoration, businessman Sano

Kichinosuke spearheaded the revival of Kaga Hōshō, pouring his private funds into the preservation of this local tradition—including the construction of what is now the Ishikawa Prefectural Noh Theater—and becoming a noh actor himself. Most of the resources available here come from Sano's collection. The museum has an active outreach program, hosting free noh and *kyōgen* classes for local schoolchildren and giving visitors a chance to try on costumes and masks.

National Noh Theatre
https://www.ntj.jac.go.jp/english/access/facilities_03.html

Located in Sendagaya, Tokyo, this important theater stages numerous performances each month (some with running commentary displayed on individual video monitors). It also features rotating exhibits, which can be viewed during intermission, and lectures that are open to the public. The theater houses a library where videos of archived performances can be viewed (for a fee, by appointment). Tickets to performances can be purchased through the theater's website.

Nogami Memorial Noh Theatre Research Institute, Hōsei University
https://nohken.ws.hosei.ac.jp/index_en.html

This institute, established in 1947 by renowned noh scholar Nogami Toyoichirō, boasts a 40,000-volume collection of precious noh-related materials. It carries out research and graduate-level education in noh studies and publishes the bulletin *Nōgaku Kenkyū*.

Tsubouchi Memorial Theatre Museum, Waseda University
https://www.waseda.jp/enpaku/en

This museum is noted particularly for its special exhibitions, which span theatrical and cinematic genres, but its permanent collection of noh materials, including valuable sound recordings and videos, is also worth exploring.

Research Institute for Japanese Traditional Music,
Kyoto City University of Arts
https://www.kcua.ac.jp/en/rijtm/

I work here as a visiting professor, teaching an introductory class on noh. The institute collaborates with Stanford University on a research project called Noh as Intermedia, which has an excellent website in English (http://noh.stanford.edu).

Off the Beaten Track

Some of noh's most fascinating traditions, exciting performances, and historic stages are to be found in Japan's regional communities. A trip to such sites (perhaps in the company of fellow students) is bound to leave a deep and lasting impression and greatly enrich your noh experience.

Tsuruoka in Yamagata prefecture hosts a Kurokawa Noh festival each February, showcasing a local tradition dating back over five hundred years. Performed mainly in farmhouses by actors from the small village of Kurokawa, the spectacle lasts all night long. Because of the venue, however, tickets can be hard to come by. The city of Matsue in Shimane prefecture is known for Sada Shin Noh, a form of sacred dancing that acquired noh-like features over time.

The Mori Butai Noh Theater in Toyoma, Miyagi prefecture, is a beautiful open-air stage designed by architect Kuma Kengo and built with local wood. Although it is an outdoor stage, a roof covers the seating area, so that performances can be held even in the rain (see photo on page 40).

Another must-see is the stage at Nunakuma Shrine in Tomonoura, Hiroshima prefecture, built by the warlord Toyotomi Hideyoshi. With its original *kagami-ita* backdrop still intact, it has been designated an important cultural property. The stage was designed to be disassembled, shipped, and rebuilt without the use of nails.

The island of Sado (Niigata prefecture) boasts the highest concentration of noh stages in the country, including several of historic importance. Among the most famous are the stages located at the

Daizen, Suwa, and Ushio shrines; the theater belonging to the Honma family (head of the Sado Hōshō school); and the Kanai Nōgakudō. The firelight noh performances on Sado feature nationally known as well as local noh actors.

The noh stage at the Asaba inn in Shuzenji Onsen, Izu (Shizuoka prefecture), is built above a pond and is exquisitely beautiful, particularly when viewed in the evening from a guest room. The *hashigakari* passageway appears to float on the water, as befits a bridge to the world beyond.

The Kita Nōbutai at Nishi Hongan-ji temple in Kyoto is the oldest surviving noh stage in Japan and a national treasure. The *hashigakari* here is at a much sharper angle relative to the main stage than is usual today, reflecting an earlier design. Though rarely used, it was the site of a memorable 2013 performance commemorating the 650th anniversary of Zeami's birth.

Utai and *hayashi* are surprisingly popular pastimes in Hokkaidō. Japan's northernmost prefecture has two outdoor noh stages, one in the city of Otaru and the other on the grounds of Kamikawa Shrine in Asahikawa.

Takami Shrine in the city of Kitakyūshū (Fukuoka prefecture) has ancient origins, extending back nearly two millennia. Its noh stage, set against a backdrop of solemn structures, is perfect for the performance of kami noh plays.

About the Author

Yasuda Noboru is a professional noh actor specializing in *waki* roles. Born in 1956 in Chōshi, Chiba prefecture, he studied Chinese philosophy as a university student before beginning his formal training in the Shimogakari Hōshō school of noh acting. He has written, directed, and performed new pieces in the style of noh and is deeply involved in children's and adult education. Yasuda is also the author of numerous books, including *Nō ni manabu shintai gihō* (Learning Body Movement from Noh) and *Ikai o tabi suru nō: Waki to iu sonzai* (Noh's Journey into the World Beyond: The Role of the *Waki*).

About the Translator

Kawamoto Nozomu is a Japanese-English translator and noh actor living in Tokyo. He grew up in New York and graduated from the University of Chicago in 1984 with a degree in anthropology. He has worked as a translator and writer for the *Mainichi Daily News* and *Japan Echo* magazine and is currently an editor/translator at the Tokyo Foundation for Policy Research. He began studying noh in 1988 and joined the Kanze school (Umewaka-kai) as a professional *shite* actor in 2002.

（英文版）能 650年 続いた仕掛けとは
Nō: 650-nen tsuzuita shikake to wa

2021年3月27日　第1刷発行

著　者　安田 登
訳　者　河本 望
発行所　一般財団法人出版文化産業振興財団
　　　　〒101-0051 東京都千代田区神田神保町2-2-30
　　　　電話　03-5211-7283
　　　　ホームページ　https://www.jpic.or.jp/

印刷・製本所　大日本印刷株式会社